STEAM IN THE LANDSCAPE

STEAM IN THE LANDSCAPE

by

K. WESTCOTT JONES

photographs by

A. J. HUDSON

BLANDFORD PRESS
POOLE   DORSET

First Published in 1971
Reprinted 1976
© 1971 Blandford Press Ltd,
Link House, West Street, Poole, Dorset BH15 1 LL

ISBN 0 7137 0542 6

Colour section printed by 4 colour sheet fed photogravure
by D. H. Greaves Ltd, Scarborough.
Text Computer Typeset in 10 pt Photon Plantin, printed and
bound by Butler & Tanner Ltd, Frome and London

CONTENTS

Aberdeen, 1965: the author admires the famous A4 Kingfisher *heading a Perth train (see pages 166–7).*

PREFACE

A considerable number of railway authorities and railwaymen have aided the author and photographer to make this book possible and to them thanks are due. There is an *esprit de corps* and a warmth among real railwaymen in all countries west and east and their ready help for the outsider who shows interest is a touching factor in international relations. The last ten years have not been easy nor happy for genuine railwaymen in a number of countries, especially in Britain, where business efficiency experts from far outside transport have taken charge of sections of an industry for which they have no feeling.

Our particular gratitude is accorded to Mr W. G. Thorpe, now Deputy Chairman and Chief Executive (Railways) of British Railways Board, notably for the facilities he made available as described on pages 166 and 167 when he was General Manager of the Scottish Region. Those people with an affection for the railway scene appreciate Mr Thorpe's remarks at Derby early in 1970 when he stated in a speech that steam was withdrawn from action on the lines of Britain too suddenly and without adequate planning for the future. Had Mr Thorpe been in a position to enforce his views a decade ago, some of the scenes depicted in this book might not have passed so quickly into history.

INTRODUCTION

For well over a century generations of young people grew up with an acceptance and even appreciation of the steam railway as a fundamental part of the landscape. The sight of a plume of steam across the fields and the unmistakable shriek of a whistle in the distance was as natural and somehow as comforting as the song of birds in the branches. The hiss of steam at a station was a friendly, familiar sound, even if small children sometimes became alarmed and covered their ears when an engine blew off noisily under the great roof of a terminal.

It was not only in Britain, founder of steam and the mother country of railways, that trains were part and parcel of the everyday scene. Out on the wintry prairies of Canada and the United States, the distinctive steam whistle of a locomotive blowing a long 'Q' for a grade crossing sounded for many miles across the wide treeless plains at night, spelling home for every North American. Today the raucous blaring horn of a diesel, if indeed trains still run on the decaying tracks across the prairies, is no substitute for that much-loved steam sound. Both American and Canadian railways know this and in response to demand after demand from lonely people manning the great wheat farms of the mid-continent, they are spending a great deal of money trying to develop a whistle for use by diesel engines that will again remind regional dwellers of the friendly railway. They are a long way from success, but to be fair, America's Northern Pacific and Canada's Canadian National have recaptured the sound to a certain extent. Even if they reproduce it exactly in years to come, however, the sight will be missing. If those happy plumes of steam cannot be seen, there is a tendency for people to act on the 'out of sight, out of mind' principle. Many believe this is a root cause of the mass desertion from rail travel in North America.

The pastoral valleys of France and Germany, too, were natural rights of way for the steam engine, although in those countries the emphasis was more on smoke than on steam. It was really only in England and Wales, especially on the lines of the former Great Western Railway, where the plume of steam was pure white. Thanks to selected, high-quality Welsh steam coal, once so cheap and easily obtainable, allied to a skill acquired through generations of experienced teaching and a pride in what used to be an eagerly-sought job of craftsmanship, engine crews controlled the combustion and the pressures so that dirty smoke was almost unknown. The railways of foreigners smoked while those of Britain steamed, or so the British thought in those days when it was fashionable to be patriotic. There is no doubt whatever, though, that British steam railways in the golden years from the turn of the century to the start of the Second World War were the pride and joy of Britons and the envy of the world.

The great thing about steam and its place in the landscape, the towns, the industrial valleys, and above the mean rooftops of city slums, was its constancy. This was one changeless thing in a changing world. Sail might disappear from the seas, and coal-burning ships give way to oil and motor engines; horses might disappear from the roads and be replaced by cars and lorries; man might learn to fly in heavier-than-air machines and his early biplanes would give way to sleek four-engined airliners, like Constellations, carrying 50 and even 80 people across the world, . . . but steam on the railways was still there. The difference between Stephenson's *Rocket* of 1829 and the streamlined A4 Class Pacifics Sir Nigel Gresley introduced in 1935 was one of degree only - they both burned coal, boiled water and made steam.

A male child born in 1870 grew up to accept - and often to love - steam engines. He accepted them as natural and as a prime means of transport. If he lived to the ripe age of 80, dying in 1950, steam was not only still there at his death but was still the prime mover of the main transport system. His country was rejoicing in the great new steam engines its newly nationalised railways were about to build and exhibit proudly at the Festival of Britain as 'Britannias'. His long lifetime would have been steadied by that one unshifting rock of sanity, the reliable, friendly, handsome steam engine. That great statesman Sir Winston Churchill lived to be 90; yet his first journey when a few weeks old was behind a steam engine, which in 1874 bore him away from his Oxfordshire birthplace; and his last journey, in a coffin, was behind a still active steam engine in regular use on the Southern Region (albeit a Battle of Britain Class Pacific named after him) which took him back to his last resting place near to where he was born. In 1965, when Sir Winston Churchill died, there were as many steam engines on the rails of Britain (about 8,000) as there were when he was born.

The dramatic and – to many of us – disastrous change took place between 1965 and 1968, when steam faded rapidly from the British railway scene. This demise had been foreshadowed by a White Paper published early in 1955 which told us that steam was eventually doomed, to be replaced by diesel traction as a 'stop gap' measure, but later by electrification. According to the White Paper, steam would recede gradually, and by 1970 few engines would remain. The then Chairman of the British Transport Commission, Sir Brian Robertson, made it quite clear that he regretted this and he not only paid tribute to steam for a century and more of sterling work but said we must never forget the romance of the 'Iron Horse'. In the White Paper he is quoted as saying that the sight of steam in the countryside and the spectacle of an express engine at night with a flickering glow from a well-stoked fire was part of our heritage. The universal affection for steam engines would, he hoped, be passed on in some measure to their successors.

But the 'Modernisation Scheme' of 1955 cost more and more money and produced greater and greater losses. The railways were taken over by iconoclasts and operated by non-professionals, sometimes businessmen called from other jobs. Steam was blamed for everything, particularly the losses, and the management actually went on record as saying that once steam was eliminated the railways would be out of the red. So the end of steam was hastened, and engines were scrapped at a faster rate than the original White Paper called for. The last main-line steam engine was withdrawn from British Railways in August 1968, leaving the system with a total of three locomotives, all narrow-gauge tanks working on the scenic Vale of Rheidol 1' 11"-gauge line from Aberystwyth to Devil's Bridge. If the statement that steam was responsible for all losses remains true, then these three engines cost British Railways £148 millions in 1969.

The steam denigrators in senior positions on the British Railways Board (successor to the British Transport Commission and the Railway Executive) have done their utmost to prevent working engines from being visible. Although 539 steam locomotives have been preserved in one form or another, only *Flying Scotsman,* privately owned by a Mr Alan Pegler, was able to run over the tracks of British Railways. This was due to a tight and binding contract Mr Pegler signed in 1963, which expired in 1972. Now several steam engines are able to achieve an airing on B.R. tracks but only after a hard struggle by the Return to Steam movement. When the graceful Pacific steamed out of Kings Cross with specials, Mr Pegler being on the footplate, tens of thousands of people came to watch. All the way to Newcastle the spectators were thick beside the tracks, and it has been estimated that more than half a million turned out to see her on the epic run to Edinburgh in 1968 when she repeated the non-stop success of forty years earlier. BBC Television filmed this, and by overwhelming demand, the film was repeated twice at peak viewing times. Such is the lure of steam.

This book tries to recapture some of the scenes which we all took for granted only a few years ago, when steam engines could be seen all day long – and for much of the night, on main lines – and when a visit to a busy station yielded the sight of half a dozen engines inside thirty minutes. This was still possible at places like Bournemouth and Stockport, Basingstoke and Barrow-in-Furness as recently as the end of 1966. Today the news that a single steam engine might be seen brings multitudes, many with tears in their eyes. Nothing, not even the sailing ship, has suffered such a rapid transformation from profusion to rarity. It does pinpoint yet again the old adage that we only appreciate something once it is gone.

Fortunately, there are some preserved railway lines worked by enthusiasts on which steam can still be seen and savoured. The white plumes of smoke are not yet vanished from the Sussex countryside for the Bluebell Railway functions over $4\frac{1}{2}$ miles of track near Horsted Keynes. Nor is it gone from glorious Devon, where the Dart Valley Railway has been rejuvenated and now runs with a success it never knew under the Western Region's management. Yorkshire has three lines in action, one in the centre of Leeds (the Middleton Railway) which allows that once familiar steam – and smoke as well – to rise above the grimy roofs of an industrial area. The Keighley and Worth Valley is another excellent private line, much sought after for locations by film makers, where steam reigns among the Yorkshire hills. More lines are being preserved as money (never easy to raise in the huge quantities demanded by British Railways for the rights which they themselves neglected) comes in for track and engines. In Wales there are seven narrow-gauge lines, all steam, contributing hugely to the tourist economy, and no one doubts these will carry on steaming beyond the year 2000.

But all steam in action in Britain (and America for that matter) at the present time is exceptional, requiring a specific effort to observe. It is special and it draws the crowds, rather like a veteran car race. A decade ago steam was natural, taken for granted, the sight of a steam-hauled express train as familiar as a car in the street or cows in a field. Erosion had set in, though, not only because of the prophecies of the White Paper. A complete change took place in management on the railways in 1961, influenced, some say, by Treasury officials, in which the operating side lost pride of place to commercial interests, and in which the need to save money tended to prevail over security, goodwill and even safety. That is why dirty engines in poor condition feature so often in the pages of this book. They had become a normal sight during the dying years, when management was inclined to despise steam. A clean engine was rather a rarity on some regions during the early sixties, and I have seen a couple of businessmen waiting on a Surrey station clap with delight when an express went through hauled by a gleaming West Country Pacific just out from the shops after an overhaul.

Many enthusiasts and railwaymen called the period between 1955 and 1960 the 'Decent Years'. This was a time when management, much of it still professional and strongly leavened with survivors of the old companies, tried hard to pay tribute to the steam scene which they knew was doomed. This was when Great Western colours were restored to express trains on the Western Region, when engines shone from frequent cleaning, and veteran types were given their last chance to 'have a go' – as with the famous *City of Truro* brought from York Railway Museum to work branch-line trains out of Newbury and Didcot. The coming of Dr Beeching in 1961 ended all that and men who were not professionals took over much of the management. The industry began to run down.

The newcomers blamed steam, and protested they could not get men to work on the railways. Old-time railwaymen, whose hearts were in their jobs and whose loyalty was such a strong point of safe and successful operation, regretted the fact that they could not get into management. It is important to remember that steam engines themselves extracted a devotion and loyalty from the master craftsmen who worked them. Footplatemen were, for a hundred years, the most admired and respected artisans in the land, and it was traditional that every boy wanted to become an engine driver.

Today, highly efficient electric engines work successfully on some main lines and no one who has the future of railways at heart would in any way decry them. They use native fuel, they are clean and quiet and immensely powerful. They have transformed timings on the London to Birmingham, Stoke, Manchester and Liverpool lines. But few boys want to grow up to be their drivers. The men who handle these machines are modern technocrats, no longer glamorous – if grimy – figures working with their hands and hearts to get the best out of a locomotive that seemed to have a personality of its own. The electric drivers push the right buttons, they have unsurpassed knowledge of the route and they have the rudiments of electric theory as well as practice learned on expensive training simulators, but somehow they have lost status. The aristocrats of the track have vanished with the steam engines they loved. To be fair, though, the high-speed electric trains of Japan's New Tokaido and New Sanyo Lines, with their 110 m.p.h. averages, have attracted the yearnings of small Japanese boys, more of whom want to be 'untenshi's' (electric train commanders) than jet pilots.

Diesel engines, of which British Railways alone have some 4,000 of many different classes, have fallen between two stools and are thoroughly unpopular with the public. Reliability is sometimes questionable, pollution from their exhausts is causing concern, and the fuel they burn is imported. Always intended as a 'stop gap' measure, they are still with us, pushing up the losses and a visible manifestation of more than £1,000,000,000 wasted on 'modernisation'. Their place in the landscape always seems alien, they attract little or no interest even from small boys who cannot remember steam in regular action but still want steam models, and their initial costs are so high they rarely repay investment in their short existence. No pictures of them will be found in this book; for they play no part, despite their gradual appearance on the railway scene from 1959 onwards, in the theme of nostalgia and recollection of how things were such a short time ago.

All is not lost for the enthusiast who travels far and wide to see steam in action. Some countries have retained big fleets of steam engines for working both passenger and freight traffic – India, South Africa, East Africa, and some Eastern European nations in particular. One railway in Southern Africa, The Benguela Company, is entirely steam-worked by 109 superbly maintained engines of various classes. Dieseliers have only now succeeded in selling the Benguela Company their products; resistance has kept them out because, as a Company chronicler has gone on record as saying, 'we have no wish to transform our "immoral" profits from steam into contemporary and fashionable losses from "modern technology" '. It is a fact that on most lines throughout the world where water, native fuel, and reasonable supplies of labour are available, steam makes a profit and diesels lose money. Most graphs in such areas show, after substitution for steam of diesel traction, a notable downturn in revenue, especially on the passenger side, almost the sole exception being the 47-mile run between Glasgow and Edinburgh. Again to be fair, substitution of electric traction almost invariably sends the graphs upwards.

In this book some pictures will be found of steam in foreign landscapes where it may be expected to continue as part of the scene for a few years yet. Even Germany has steam engines in regular use, while Czechoslovakia has a comparatively modern steam fleet of well over 3,000 locomotives. The Trans-Siberian Railway is being electrified throughout, but huge 4–8–4 steam engines work passenger trains on the eastern section between Lake Baikal and Khabarovsk, then down towards the Siberian Pacific coast. It will be 1976 or even 1977 before they disappear completely, but meanwhile they are maintained in very fine condition, painted green and cream – not red as some might expect. I travelled the Trans-Siberian Railway in 1969, recording the longest continuous steam journey (more than 2,200 miles) that I have ever known in a year when that colourful means of traction had already disappeared from so many parts of the world. It is a reminder, as are some of Tony Hudson's photographs ranging from Chile to East Africa, that steam – or at least smoke – is still a natural and accepted part of some remote landscapes wilder than our own pastoral and industrial scene which misses it so nostalgically.

ties and governments of Eastern Europe where so much living steam is housed. In those countries, it is dictated that conventional art is the only proper form for socialists and left-wing intellectuals to enthuse about, with the result that lovers of steam engines seen photographing or sketching them are sometimes arrested and suspected of spying! There is evidence, however, that some realisation of the treasures still to be found on the railways of such countries as Romania, Czechoslovakia, Hungary, Poland, Bulgaria and Yugoslavia is becoming apparent.

Let us translate *Flying Scotsman*'s visual attractions into performance on the track, remembering that this aesthetic machine endowed with a kind of life by coal and fire and the devoted skill of two pairs of hands is a 'locomotive', that is to say, capable of moving herself and a load at a forward speed. *Flying Scotsman* was the first British steam locomotive officially recorded at a speed of 100 m.p.h., this figure being measured in a dynamometer car attached to the tender. The run was on 30 November 1934, when the engine was eleven years old, and it was made to establish the possibilities of high-speed trains to mark the Silver Jubilee of King George V. It is true that the Great Western 4-4-0, *City of Truro*, when hurtling down from Whiteball Summit in Somerset with the 'Ocean Liner Express' in 1904, attained a speed of $102\frac{1}{2}$ m.p.h., but this was recorded on the footplate by Mr Charles Rous-Marten. *City of Truro*'s great speed is accepted as the first 'century' in Britain, which is why the handsome locomotive is preserved in Swindon Railway Museum, but the actual figure can only be a strong claim, not a scientifically recorded fact. With *Flying Scots-*

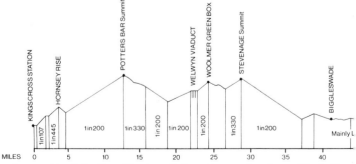

Gradient profile of the Great Northern Railway between London and Stoke Sum *ilthough the long climb to Stoke is against the engine for 15 miles and has bee*

man the speed was shown a dozen times over by delicate instruments studied by a team of experts at the time of running in the specially-equipped dynamometer car. Driver Sparshatt of immortal memory was at the throttle and Fireman Webster was on the shovel when this 100-m.p.h. reading was obtained running down from Stoke Summit, and the speed was held for a minute. On that test run, the great footplate team, whose names were as well known to legions of rail fans in the 1930s as footballers are to the crowds of the 1970s, coaxed *Flying Scotsman* to run at 90 m.p.h. for no less than 40 miles.

In August 1927, *Flying Scotsman* hauled the inaugural non-stop train from Kings Cross over the 268 miles to Newcastle. Her load was eight coaches of 293 tons and the schedule was five and a half hours, the timing for the first 100 miles to the Summit of Stoke Bank being 105 minutes. Almost exactly forty years later the same engine celebrated this occasion by setting out from Kings Cross with a train for Newcastle weighing 387 tons. By this time, *Flying Scotsman* belonged to Mr Alan Pegler, but he had the support of many well-wishing railwaymen below Board level and every attempt was made to offer a clear path.

In the event, a points failure at Tuxford North signal box, 131 miles North of London, brought the train – and all trains on the Eastern Region main line – to a halt for 38 minutes. In all, 46 minutes were lost due to slowing, waiting and starting from this permanent-way fault, but even so the train (heavier than the 1927 version) was brought to Newcastle in 316 minutes, nine minutes quicker than the scheduled and actual times of forty years ago.

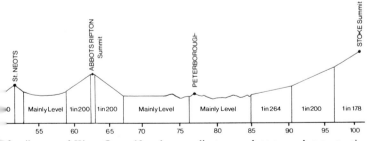

0 miles out of Kings Cross. Note how gradients were kept to modest proportions
mous testing ground for more than 100 years of steam operation.

Taking the net time as 265 minutes, the gain to the veteran engine was amazing.

As a passenger aboard the train, riding in the third coach, I timed *Flying Scotsman* on this 1967 journey and later rode on her footplate, having walked through the corridors of the twin tenders to an invited place on the bucking engine as we pounded through Darlington. Log 1 (page 31) shows that for the first 100 miles to Stoke Summit (the gradient diagram is shown on pages 20 and 21) we took 100 minutes, 45 seconds, some $4\frac{1}{4}$ minutes faster than the schedule of 40 years before. A top speed of 87 m.p.h. was achieved coming down towards Biggleswade. A feature of the run was that the numerous water troughs once provided along the line in the days of steam had all been removed, apart from two, and so it was essential to collect a good supply of water from each of these, requiring a rather slower speed than usual. Coal, too, had to be loaded aboard from merchants' lorries and not from railway hoists, and this required some caution towards the end of the run as the supplies appeared to be running very low in the main tender. *Flying Scotsman* is equipped with two tenders these days, in order to overcome the water problem, but the second tender (taken from a Gresley A4) is only a water tank; all coal supplies are stored in the first – original – tender.

When I reached the cab of the engine shortly before Darlington, steam pressure was visibly falling and there was a worried look on the faces of the comparatively large number of persons riding the footplate. The official driver, the official fireman, a volunteer fireman, a chief inspector, a divisional manager (incognito), who was taking a turn on the shovel, and Mr Alan Pegler were there, discussing what to do if the coal ran out with 36 miles to go to Newcastle. Although we slammed round the back of Darlington station at 70 m.p.h., speed soon fell off during the climb at 1 in 220/203 towards Aycliffe and Bradbury, and pressure fell to 120 pounds per square inch from the desirable level of 200 lb. There was even talk of chopping up the woodwork in the first coach and using it for fuel as a cheaper alternative than coming to a disastrous stop requiring costly rescue operations and a serious holdup of following traffic. But in fact there was more coal than the trimmers thought, and this plus dust kept pressure at a sufficient level for the engine to bring her train across the King Edward Bridge and into Newcastle Central at 1.30 p.m., 31 minutes late on the scheduled time but showing a recovery of seven minutes from the lateness following the permanent-way stop at Tuxford.

The log of *Flying Scotsman*'s performance, which should be read in conjunction with the gradient profile of the line from Kings Cross to Stoke Summit, is shown in detail up to the unfortunate obstruction at Tuxford, and thereafter, once the points failure had been repaired, in outline onwards to Newcastle, page 31 (Log 1). It is an overall tribute to an engine then 44 years old hauling a train weighing 100 tons heavier than she hauled when only four years old. If any main-line diesel engine should ever achieve the ripe old age of 44, I have grave doubts that it would manage to perform better than its specifications called for when new. This sums up the great beauty and interest of steam in action; unpredictable, capable of great things when blending with a team of devoted men, magnificent in determination and appearance.

But *Flying Scotsman* is not an exceptional locomotive despite all the publicity that surrounds her journeys. Other steam engines reappeared on our tracks, and it was seen that well-maintained locomotives were capable of feats of speed and haulage in keeping with their earlier records. Experts on the footplate can extract far more from a steam locomotive than the figures prepared by the designers might indicate. Some astonishing things have been done in the past with relatively underpowered engines, and many performances are written into history, especially during the 1888 and 1895 periods when the 'Railway Races' to Edinburgh and Aberdeen took place. Even when, as sometimes happened, a steam locomotive went lame, careful driving could coax it into action and usually the train was brought to safety where a replacement awaited. Unless the mishap was really serious, such as a collapsing firebox or coupling rods falling off (these things happened during the latter days of steam operation in Britain due to bad maintenance and official neglect), an engine could be persuaded to limp along. There was little or no abandonment of trains miles from anywhere, as happens all too frequently with diesel traction.

People who do not recall the halcyon days of steam, essentially pre-war but still fair and sunny until about 1955, tend to regard steam as a denigrated means of traction because official policy thundered on against it. Propaganda, often underwritten by oil and motor interests, did untold damage, and railway practices in the early sixties were so shameful that many of the best and most devoted men either lost heart or left the service. Deliberate actions, or near criminal neglect, were responsible for much of the deterioration among steam engines still on main-line service.

The run-down of steam coal supplies accounts in part for the withering of steam locomotive performance. There was a time when coal was specially selected for those engines rostered for the named expresses, and it was by no means unknown for drivers and firemen to reject a tender-full of coal. On the Great Western Railway, where the engines and their grates were designed for the best Welsh steam coal, it was rare for any failures to occur and amazingly heavy loads could be handled by locomotives of modest size. Log 2 (page 32) shows a

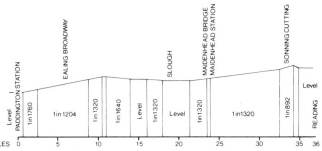

Gradient profile of Brunel's masterpiece, the Great Western Railway, showing how he achieved the most perfect level and near level system in the world. Built between Paddington and Reading in 1837–8, it remains unaltered and the bridge over the Thames at Maidenhead is still the longest brick arch bridge in the world.

run from Paddington to Reading which I made in late October 1936, with Star Class 4-6-0 No. 4035, *Queen Charlotte*. This was a Star designed by Churchward and built early in 1907; thus in its twenty-ninth year it was on main-line runs, and when I encountered this gleaming, shapely engine it stood at the head of a train of 16 coaches, weighing more than 560 tons loaded. The express was the 3.15 p.m. 'afternoon-tea train' to Oxford and Worcester, which in the 1930s, with negligible road competition, was always full.

Queen Charlotte, as will be seen from the log, not only kept time but was fractionally ahead, driven to standard Great Western practice. Today, higher speeds are attained by diesels on such limited trains as the 'Cornish Riviera' and the 'Golden Hind' but the weight is limited to eight coaches of new light steel construction, weighing perhaps 285 tons loaded. A Star, even after thirty years of work, thought nothing of twice this load. Computers and economists can perhaps illuminate how the economic balance is in favour of today's train, but all I can say is that the Star cost £14,000 against the diesels' £260,000, and that the Great Western Railway paid a dividend to its private shareholders from profits genuinely earned.

Log 3 (page 32) shows another Great Western run, dating from 1937, and this one illustrates the average running to Taunton by a typical Saturday express in summer. The date was 31 July and the train, a very heavy one of 18 coaches including first- and third-class restaurant cars, was fully loaded, every seat being taken, while baggage was stacked in the guards van and on all racks. The gross weight was reckoned at 640 tons, but the single engine heading the train was No. 4084, one of the original Castles of 1923–24, a 4–6–0 of comparatively modest proportions. A minute was lost on the schedule of 160 minutes for the 143 miles to Taunton, but as a signal stop had halted the train at milepost 119, the net time for the run was only 156 minutes, showing a gain to the locomotive of four minutes.

Such performances were commonplace in pre-war days, and the engines as well as coaches were spotlessly clean. It is difficult for anyone not able to remember the pre-war period to understand the situation, especially as they have been bombarded with 'modernisation' and 'rationalisation' propaganda. Historical facts just have to speak for themselves, even if the subsequent decline can be justified as being due to a reduction in the 'labour-intensive' side of railway operation, decline in quality of coal, soaring costs, and a legacy of war-time over-use of equipment. During the war, the demands made on engine power rose to incredible proportions, and trains on the main lines from London to Newcastle and Carlisle were frequently made up of 21 coaches, and even of 26 on occasion. Owing to the Forces' requirements, there were fewer men for maintenance, and speed limits were set at 65 m.p.h. Double and even treble stops were required at intermediate stations, so lateness even on the modified schedules occurred fairly often. Packed compartments, slower journeys, reduced standards of cleanliness, elimination of restaurant cars, the blackout, and less frequent services all led to making rail trips purgatory for many on the main lines between 1940 and 1945.

After the war, starved of capital and faced with impending nationalisation, the private railway companies could do little to restore pre-war conditions. But even so, standards of maintenance and the general cleanliness of trains was far higher in the 1946–47 period than ten or even twenty years later, and a better *esprit de corps* was apparent among the railway staffs. The early years of nationalisation were not unsatisfactory, and until 1952 the railways made a comfortable profit: Unrestricted road-freight competition and the lifting of petrol rationing hit the railways hard, coupled with desertions due to the recent memories of war-time journeys by the private traveller, now finding a new and apparently happy freedom to motor at will.

Then came the fruitless 'modernisation' plans by both new and old railway officials suddenly armed with Government loan money to spend. They were perhaps pressed by outside interests, particularly by those selling another kind of fossil fuel, and mistakes were made which escalated. Steam was denigrated and allowed to waste away, and if it had not been for devoted bands of men in the surviving sheds keeping locomotives in action, there might have been some serious disasters. Nevertheless, throughout the period 1955–67, during which the number of steam engines declined from 18,800 to under 200, remarkable performances were kept up by steam-hauled trains, despite every kind of discouragement. In 1962 there was even rivalry for the 'World's Fastest Steam Train' between the crews working the 5.30 p.m. Oxford to Paddington express and a Paris (Est) to Basle express, both of which averaged 63·5 m.p.h. But although Oxford dons keenly followed the progress of these trains, and the firemen actually exchanged letters, the rivalry was ended when management slowed the Oxford train by five minutes and required a stop at Didcot. But for such a title to be claimed in 1962 for 63·5 m.p.h. contrasts sadly with the G.W.R. claim of 71·4 m.p.h. with its *Cheltenham Flier* thirty years earlier.

Where, now, is the 'World's Fastest Steam Train'? Is there an express regularly hauled by steam traction that can make such a claim? Conditions change so rapidly that at the time of going to press those expresses still qualifying may be diesel-hauled in a few days. But in the spring of 1974 it is fair to suggest that for at least another year contenders will be as widespread as the 'Taj Express' from Delhi to Agra in India, the 'Orange Express' between Kimberley and De Aar in South Africa, and the 'Balt-Orient Express' between Cseska-Trebova and Brno in Czechoslovakia. None of these trains average more than 48 to 50 m.p.h., but they are quite heavy and the steam in action heading them makes a splendid spectacle. West and East Germany still have many fast trains hauled by steam engines of various classes, and this is the region most likely to offer frequent bursts of 60 m.p.h. or more, but overall averages with steam traction will be below 50 m.p.h. since the duties are largely secondary involving many stops en route. Until the spring of 1972 occasional heavy expresses west-bound from Angers in France, especially relief trains at holiday periods, may have secured a mammoth 4–8–2 of the 241P Class, in which case the schedule onwards to Nantes or to Le Mans called for just over 60 m.p.h., but no one could be sure of such a rostering. New Zealand has enjoyed its last winter with main-line steam, when the heroic Ja Class 4-6-2s on South Island hurtled over the 3′ 6″-gauge track from Christchurch to Oamaru at an average of 51 m.p.h. with maximum speeds often 65 and above. Unfortunately, none of the numerous privately-run enthusiast lines in Britain, America and Europe has sufficient track or sufficient power to offer steam speeds in excess of about 40 m.p.h.

To see steam in action in the early seventies is not difficult but must inevitably be costly unless one lives close to an enthusiast's line. West Germany is the most certain venue, followed by Eastern Europe, while the African Continent, India, Java and Japan (to say nothing of mainland China) have huge fleets. One railway which is all steam is the Benguela in Angola, and it must be classed as the most delightful system still extant. Primarily a line for bringing copper down from the Congo and Northern Zambia through 878 miles of high-altitude tropical Africa to the coast at Benguela and Lobito, the Benguela Railway is an Anglo-Portuguese concern, uses 109 steam engines and makes a very satisfactory profit. There are passenger trains, and the first class coaches are among the best kept and most comfortable in the world today, in a somewhat period style, while the restaurant cars recall the finest in pre-war rail travel with meals at low prices and wines served in silver coolers. Facing a tremendous climb from Benguela up the coastal escarpment for 68 miles to Cubral on a gradient of 1 in 40, steam is seen in action in its finest form. Much of the mileage is covered by wood-burning engines, using the hard eucalyptus grown in plantations by the trackside for hundreds of miles. Thermal efficiency by this means is surprisingly high.

There are many people, experts among them, who believe that steam traction was never developed to its fullest possible extent. It is no use comparing the performances of steam engines developed thirty or more years ago with electric, diesel-electric, or diesel-mechanical engines built within the past two years, although in fact the steam engines show up remarkably well once in motion with heavy loads. Where diesels start with more adhesion and gather speed more rapidly, the steam locomotives (even those forty years old) hold a fast pace with a heavier load. But so many innovations could have been applied to new generations of steam engines if scientists, politicians, and major industrial interests had been willing to create them. An invention by Dr Giesl-Gieslingen of Vienna produced spectacular results in thermal efficiency. The 'Giesl Ejector', fitted in place of a conventional chimney, is a sort of 'jet-pump' for inducing draught in steam boilers, and it prevents waste of energy. The exhaust is softened and the locomotive's efficiency is increased by 8% to 21% according to type.

Dr Giesl-Gieslingen, a lecturer at Vienna Technological University, studied in Philadelphia for many years and was associated with locomotive engineering on the eastern seaboard and in Austria. His oblong-shaped Ejector has changed the appearance of the front end of several thousand engines since the late 1950s and made its way to Britain where it was experimentally fitted to a Battle of Britain Class Pacific of the Southern Region and a 9F Class 2-10-0 of the London Midland Region. Both were remarkably successful, as is shown by reports issued from the motive power departments, but there it would appear that the results were hushed up and questions asked in Parliament were muffled by evasive replies. British Railways were said at that stage to be too committed to dieselisation (in 1962) to consider any revolutionary change in steam motive power. It is known from papers, however, that the Battle of Britain's thermal efficiency increased by 14% during a year of running fitted with a Giesl Ejector.

Nevertheless, some 3,000 modern engines in Czechoslovakia have subsequently been fitted, and the invention has gone round the world wherever steam survives in strength. Even the big Garratts of the East African Railways, pictures of which appear in this book, have now been fitted, with a consequent improvement in performance. If the British Railways trials were 'sabotaged', as has been suggested, at least the Ejectors appeared to advantage on engines of the National

Coal Board and the Talyllyn Railway. In Dr Giesl-Gieslingen's own country all remaining steam engines carry his Ejector. It is ironic that Austria also gave birth to another inventor, Rudolf Diesl (1858-1913), whose oil engine did not appear in strength until some twenty years after his death. In 1963 there were actually headlines in the railway press on the lines of 'Giesl beats Diesl'. But already it was too late.

As history must now be written, it will apppear that maximum development in steam traction took place in the years 1935-41. This was when Sir Nigel Gresley built his wonderful streamlined A4 Pacifics which took charge of such trains as the streamlined 'Silver Jubilee' and 'Coronation' and achieved a regular daily run of six hours for the $393\frac{3}{4}$ miles between Kings Cross and Edinburgh. It is fair to point out that 25 minutes have been taken off this timing rather more than thirty years later by the Deltic diesel-hauled 'Flying Scotsman' running at about the same weight, an improvement of just over 7% gained at an outlay of at least £80 millions in traction and track relaying. In the United States the famous 'Hiawatha' expresses were running between Chicago, Milwaukee, and the Twin Cities at point-to-point averages of 84 m.p.h. behind Milwaukee Railroad high-wheeled 4-6-2s. This was the fastest train in the world at the time, and hundreds of people used to come down to the trackside every day just to watch the 'Hiawatha' pass. In 1940-41, the American Union Pacific Railroad put into service their gigantic 'Big Boy' articulated engines, capable of hauling 5,000 tons unaided over the heavy grades of the Rocky Mountain section between Cheyenne and Laramie. These were, and will undoubtedly remain, the largest steam engines ever built.

No one with the interests of rail transport at heart would in any way denigrate electric traction and the benefits it brings, with fast acceleration, quiet, fume-free progress, intense usage, clean maintenance, and high sustained speeds. Electric traction first appeared in 1883; but it is still capable of development, as the Japanese are showing with their New Sanyo Line, an extension of the highly successful New Tokaido Line built in 1962-65. British Railways have wisely elected to put the whole of their Euston-Glasgow route under live wires, a project which should be completed by 1974. The most desirable electrification schemes are those which employ natural water power, as in Switzerland, but so long as a native fuel such as coal can be used in the power stations to feed the live wires, electric trains have a tremendous advantage over all others.

It may be that new forms of traction will take shape and expand, such as the aero-train, advanced passenger trains employing gas turbines, and hover-trains running above concrete tracks on a cushion of air. But one thing is clear. Diesel traction has been merely an alternative method to steam, scarcely improving on it from the point of view of performance and alienating many supporters of the railway. In a few desert areas, notably the Kalahari Desert of southern Africa, the Nullarbor Plain of Australia, and the arid lands of the south-west United States, where oil is as easy or easier to come by as coal, and water – that vital ingredient of steam traction – is totally lacking, diesels have transformed the economics and will continue as prime traction for many years to come. In settled and highly populated regions diesel traction should be forced to give way as soon as possible to electrification, and where labour, suitable fuels, and water are readily available at low cost, steam traction should be retained and even extended.

If this book helps in any way to pay long overdue tributes to steam, the harnessing of which, when applied to railways, proved to be mankind's most important and progressive invention, it will have served some purpose. If it redresses some of the wrongs done to steam engines by post-war officials, and exposes some of the blatant bias which caused thousands of engines to be retired ahead of time and millions of pounds to be wasted, it will have achieved a further objective. If it reminds older readers of the joys of seeing steam in action and informs younger ones where such sights may yet be observed in a changing world, it will have succeeded in its prime intention.

PERFORMANCE LOGS

(1) KINGS CROSS TO NEWCASTLE, Saturday, 17 June 1967.
Commemorative non-stop run (40th anniversary). 'Hadrian Flyer'
hauled by No. 4472 *Flying Scotsman* A3 Class 4–6–2, former
L.N.E.R.

10 coaches, 387 tons tare, 425 tons full, including extra tender.

Miles	Station	Schedule (in minutes)	Actual Time (in minutes)	Speed (m.p.h.)
—	Kings Cross	(8.14 a.m.)	(8.14 a.m.)	—
2·5	Finsbury Park	6	9.25	37
5·0	Wood Green	—	12.45	50
			(permanent way slack)	35
9·2	New Barnet	—	18.50	48
12·7	Potters Bar	—	23.15	46
17·7	Hatfield	24	28.15	67
28·6	Stevenage	—	38.15	72
31·9	Hitchin	37	40.50	80
41·1	Biggleswade	—	47.30	88/84
51·7	St Neots	—	55.30	80/75
58·9	Huntingdon	59	61.30	74
63·5	Abbots Ripton	—	65.20	66
69·4	Holme	—	69.50	80/69
76·4	Peterborough	75	76.45	20 (slack)
84·8	Tallington	—	86.10	70
92·2	Little Bytham	—	92.40	69
100·1	Stoke Box & Summit	—	100.20	58
105·5	Grantham	105	105.00	76/70
115·4	Claypole	—	112.20	88½
120·1	Newark	117	116.00	77
131·0	Mile Post 131	—	129.10	—
138·6	Retford	133	177.50	55
156·0	Doncaster	153	195.50	56
174·4	Selby	175	213.15	50 (slack)
188·2	York	190	227.50	15 (slack)
210·4	Thirsk	212	252.30	68
218·2	Northallerton	219	259.45	62
232·3	Darlington	237	274.45	57 (slack)
245·2	Ferryhill	255	287.45	68
254·3	Durham	264	297.20	30 (slack)
268·3	Newcastle-on-Tyne	285	316.00	—

Note: A points failure at Mile Post 131 necessitated a halt of
37¼ mins, ruining the run. The author was on the footplate
between Thirsk and Darlington.

(2) PADDINGTON TO READING, Saturday, 26 October 1936.
3.15 p.m. to Oxford and Worcester, 16 coaches, 568 tons full.
Star Class 4–6–0 locomotive No. 4035, *Queen Charlotte*, Great
Western Railway.

Miles	Station	Schedule (in minutes) (3.15 p.m.)	Actual Time (in minutes) (3.15 p.m.)	Speed (m.p.h.)
—	Paddington	—	—	—
1·2	Westbourne Park	3	—	25
4·5	Acton	—	8.10	44
5·8	Ealing Broadway	8	9.50	52
11·0	Hayes & Harlington	14	16.10	56
13·2	West Drayton	16	18.30	59
14·5	Iver	—	—	66
18·5	Slough	21	23.00	64
23·2	Taplow	—	—	66
24·2	Maidenhead	27	28.30	65
31·0	Twyford	—	34.30	66
34·0	Mile Post 34	—	—	70½
36·0	Reading	40	39.45	—

(3) PADDINGTON TO TAUNTON, Saturday, 31 July 1937.
12.05 p.m. to Minehead and Ilfracombe, 18 coaches, 640 tons full.
Castle Class 4–6–0 locomotive No. 4084, *Aberystwyth Castle*, Great
Western Railway.

Miles	Station	Schedule (in minutes) (12.05 p.m.)	Actual Time (in minutes) (12.06 p.m.)	Speed (m.p.h.)
—	Paddington	—	—	—
4·5	Acton	—	8.10	48½
5·8	Ealing Broadway	9	10.00	52
9·0	Southall	—	13.50	58
13·2	West Drayton	16	18.10	65
18·5	Slough	21	23.30	60½
24·2	Maidenhead	—	28.30	76/62½
31·0	Twyford	—	—	—
36·0	Reading	38	39.30	66/35 (slack)
44·8	Aldermaston	—	49.30	56
53·0	Newbury	59	58.35	58
61·5	Hungerford	—	70.15	52½
70·0	Savernake (summit)	80	81.55	45/57
75·2	Pewsey	—	—	75
81·0	Patney	—	92.00	75
95·0	Westbury cut-off Junc.	—	—	67
106·5	Witham	—	117.30	61
111·8	Bruton (and summit)	—	—	47/26½
115·2	Castle Cary	—	131.10	31
119·0	Mile Post 119	—	Signal stop (45 secs.)	—
122·2	Charlton Mackerell	—	—	80
125·8	Somerton	—	141.50	74
135·0	Athelney	—	151.00	66
143·0	Taunton	160	161.10	—

(4) WATERLOO TO SALISBURY. Friday, 6 December 1961.
11 a.m. *Atlantic Coast Express*. 12 coaches, 405 tons tare, 430 tons full.
Merchant Navy Class Pacific 4–6–2 No. 35029, *Ellerman Line*.

Miles	Station	Schedule (in minutes)	Actual Time (in minutes)	Speed (m.p.h.)
—	Waterloo	(11 a.m.)	(11 a.m.)	—
3·9	Clapham Junction	7	7.20	40 (slack)
7·3	Wimbledon	11	11.20	58
8·6	Raynes Park	—	12.40	66
12·0	Surbiton	16	16.15	68
13·3	Hampton Court Junction	—	17.30 ⎫	(Signal stop)
		—	29.20 ⎭	(Signal failure)
17·1	Walton	—	34.15	63
24·4	Woking	28	40.15	70
33·0	Farnborough	—	47.45	72
36·3	Fleet	—	50.30	73
42·2	Hook	—	55.20	74
47·9	Basingstoke	48	60.15	70
				(after signals)
55·6	Overton	—	66.20	82
61·1	Hurstborne	—	71.15	88
66·3	Andover Junction	64	74.50	92
72·6	Grateley	—	79.45	70
80·0	Mile Post 80	—	—	86
83·8	Salisbury	80	90.00	—

The author travelled on the footplate throughout this run. Although the signal failure caused a 12-minute dead stand, the arrival in Salisbury was only 10 minutes late, and the net time recorded for the engine was only 77 minutes. The driver was E. H. Pistell and the fireman was N. Abbott, both of Salisbury Shed.

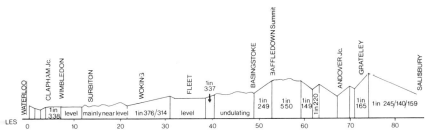

Gradient profile of the 83¾ miles of track from Waterloo to Salisbury, over the former London and South Western Railway.

1
2

▲ *Raynes Park*   ▼ *Finsbury Park*

Paddington – Subway Junction

5
6

Paddington – the Arrivals side

Betchworth

8
10

Betchworth

Charlbury

Charlbury

15

16

Honeybourne

Honeybourne

East Wales

22
23

Exeter

Haresfield (winter)

27
29

Haresfield (winter)

Haresfield (summer)

33

34

Haresfield (summer)

▲ *Shipton*   ▼ *Sudbury Hill*

35
37

36
38   ▲ *Shipton*   ▼ *Sudbury Hill*

Llanbrynmair

40

42

Llanbrynmair

Vauxhall

43
44

45

Waterloo

46

47

48

49

oo ▲

unction

Clapham Junction

52

53

Clapham Junction

Woodford Halse

54
55

West Country

Fleet – down trains

58 59

Fleet – up trains

Abergavenny

66
67

Abergavenny

Winter

68
69

Winter

Gloucester

72
73

74

75

Trelewis

Crumlin

C

in

Barnstaple

82
83

Barnstaple

Barnstaple

85
87

Barnstaple

Worcestershire

Worcestershire

Cheltenham

93

94

Cheltenham

Bromsgrove

Bromsgrove

Lickey

99
101

Lickey

Aylesbury

Ryde

Ryde

Ryde

Newport

113
114

115
116

Newport

Cowes

118

Cowes

Wroxall

Ventnor

▲ *Weybridge*

▼ *Abermule*

127
128

▲ *Sonning* ▼ *Longmoor*

Aberdeen

Aberdeen

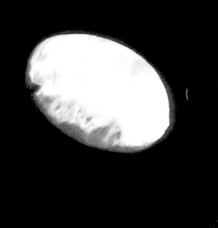

Hereford

Northern Ireland

Rouen

140
141

Rouen

Cathedrals of Steam

Cathedrals of Steam

Paris

148
149

Paris

France – 'Mountains'

France – 'Mountains'

Switzerland

Chile

Kenya

Kenya

Uganda

162
164

163

Uganda

165

166

167

Czechoslovakia

168

169

Czechoslovakia

Hungary

172
174

173

175

Hungary

Yugoslavia

178
179

Spain

Specials

Condemned

185

Saved

186

The King

DESCRIPTIONS OF THE

COLOURED ILLUSTRATIONS

Raynes Park   Pl. 1
    Typical of the thrilling sights that could be seen and enjoyed at
least every half-hour throughout the day right up to the middle of
1967 is this shot of rebuilt Merchant Navy Class Pacific No. 35012,
United States Lines, on a Southampton and Bournemouth express at
Raynes Park, Surrey. This unusual Southern Region commuter
station, with its staggered platforms giving an overall length of more
than a quarter of a mile, was a favoured vantage point for railway
enthusiasts in the early sixties. Situated $8\frac{3}{4}$ miles from Waterloo (a
distance measured to the point where the down platforms ceased and
the up ones began), Raynes Park was just beyond the inner London
60 m.p.h. speed limit, and steam expresses for the Hampshire Coast
or the Exeter Line were accelerating in the down direction. Up trains
were passing through with a final fling in the 70 m.p.h. bracket before
easing for the restriction beginning at Wimbledon.
    United States Lines carries the discs used in steam days to give an
immediate visual route indication. Those in the picture (taken in
April 1964) show the train to be taking the left hand junction at
Worting beyond Basingstoke, towards Southampton, Bournemouth
and Weymouth. The magnificent Bulleid Pacifics, introduced as
streamliners in 1941, were rebuilt in 1956–57, and flowered in their
later form with Walschaerts valve gear and air-smoothed casing
removed. No. 35012 saw service up to the last year of steam on the
Southern, being withdrawn for scrapping in August 1967 with 17
surviving sisters. Two remain intact for preservation at the present

132

time. It is rather poignant to note that *United States Lines'* withdrawal only preceded by two years the cessation of passenger trading by the great shipping line after which she was named.

Finsbury Park   Pl. 2

Steam officially perished at Kings Cross Top Shed on Saturday 15 June 1963, the day that this picture was taken. One of the superb Gresley A3 Pacifics, No. 60061 *Pretty Polly* (they were named after Derby horses), is seen in forlorn condition on a down express to Leeds running through the Eastern Region suburban station after climbing through the tunnels from Kings Cross $2\frac{1}{2}$ miles away. The A3 Class was introduced in 1927, and most of the 70 locomotives gave 35 years of splendid service on main line work. During the war they were often called upon to haul 20-coach trains out of Kings Cross. As the last engines were cleared from Top Shed it was said that enginemen who had worked there would never forget the exploits of steam, especially those with the famed A3s, never to be seen in Kings Cross again. But they were seen on many occasions after that, coming up from the North after taking over expresses from failed diesels. As late as 28 December 1963, I came up from York behind A3 *Sir Hugo*, No. 60083, in even more neglected condition than we see *Pretty Polly*, yet she held to the same timings as the defunct diesel, from whom she had rescued the train up in the North Eastern Region, was supposed to have achieved. Since *Flying Scotsman*, then owned by Mr Alan Pegler, left King's Cross on a nonstop run to Edinburgh in 1968, no main line steam engines have worked through Finsbury Park under their own power.

Paddington   Pl. 3-6

In a thick February mist we see steam activity at Subway Junction, about three quarters of a mile out from Paddington, the former Great Western Railway's London terminus. It was 1964, and steam had only another 18 months of survival on the Western Region. Pannier tanks of various classes, all 0-6-0s, still had charge of empty stock workings, while the splendid Castle Class 4-6-0s hauled expresses on the Oxford, Worcester, Hereford line. Pounding out of a murky Paddington morning, exactly on time at 11.15 a.m., we see No. 7011, *Banbury Castle*, with a restaurant-car express to Worcester. Keeping time in fog and thick mist presented no problem to the Great Western, for that company pioneered A.T.C. (Automatic Train Control) before the First

World War. A ramp between the rails repeated in the cabs of locomotives, sounding a bell if the signal was down but a hooter if it was adverse. All Western Region engines continue to use this system and it has spread in various forms to other parts of British Railways. The G.W.R. had a fantastic safety record, difficult for those brought up in an age of slaughter (especially on the roads) to understand. For 40 consecutive years the G.W.R. avoided loss of life to any passenger, and in that time they carried some 1,400 millions of them.

The other Paddington pictures show *Clifford Castle*, No. 5098, built in 1946 (and here let it be said that the Castle Class was still being built when some of the earliest examples constructed at Swindon nearly 30 years earlier were being withdrawn), steaming into Paddington with an Oxford train in April 1964 after being held outside by a signal. Up to the end of steam, most Western Region engines were kept in reasonable condition, but *Clifford Castle* was obviously not included in this.

Betchworth   Pl. 7–10

Tucked away 'round the corner' of the main Brighton line, Betchworth is a typical Surrey country station which retained its character right up to the end of steam on the Redhill-Guildford-Reading line in 1966. Only 25 miles from Victoria, Betchworth is reached by changing at Redhill or Reigate off an electric multiple unit. Until so very recently, the first stop on the Guildford line after the change took one back through the years to a happy little steam paradise. Today the line is still open, worked by diesel units which link Redhill and Reading. Of course, the whole line is an oddity – it was the South Eastern's (of all people) attack on the Brighton and South Western Companies, and by this tortuous method they reached Reading in the west.

These four pictures, taken on a sunny August day in 1963 when the pleasant afternoon sounds of a country station were the singing of birds, the buzzing of insects, an occasional clank from a signal going down, infrequent bells and the gentle chuffing of steam, show Betchworth at its best. A fairly modern Class 4MT 2–6–4 tank, built at Brighton in 1951, leaves for Redhill with a Reading train. Below it we see quite the ugliest class of steam locomotive ever designed – Bulleid's functional Q1 'Austerity' 0–6–0s introduced in 1942 – taking a freight through on its way to Redhill. Despite their raw appearance these Q1s had a fantastic turn of speed, and on the line between Lenham and Ashford in 1943 a special trip showing them off to the Transport Press of wartime produced a horrific and utterly illegal 90 m.p.h. In plate 10 we see a U Class 2–6–0 Southern 'Mogul' dating from 1928 coming into Betchworth with a Reading train. The engine is passing over the level crossing which in those days was properly manned; the traditional South Eastern and Chatham Railway lattice-work signal is of interest.

Charlbury   Pl. 11–14

Water troughs were once a natural part of the railway scene, something we took for granted on country stretches of line where engines could be refreshed without stopping. Like most things to do with railways they were a British invention dating from 1859 (North Wales) and they enabled us to run trains over long distances without stopping. Charlbury Troughs were a mile west of the small Oxfordshire town, 78 miles from Paddington on the line to Worcester. They succoured engines until the end of 1965 before being ripped out because diesels are not normally in need of transit water.

Laid between the tracks on a perfectly level stretch, troughs varied in length but those at Charlbury were half a mile long, slightly less than average. To pick up water, the fireman used to let down a scoop and the driver slowed to an optimum speed of between 45 and 60 m.p.h. Going too fast over the troughs produced a very spectacular – and sometimes dangerous – spray from beneath the tender, which has been known to break carriage windows. In these pictures we see in plate 11 a Worcester train on the Charlbury Troughs (looking towards Oxford), and a Class 4 mixed-traffic 4–6–0 of British Railways design, built in 1952. To the right of the tracks the big tank for filling the troughs can be clearly observed. These are summer scenes and in good, dry, warm weather (not unknown in the Oxfordshire countryside) water troughs need a great deal of topping up after thirsty engines have passed over them. A close view of the Class 4 No. 75022 (plate 12), heading a short pick-up freight, indicates the engine is probably not taking water since such a train would make frequent stops and avail itself of the flexible hoses which used to grace the ends of most station platforms. On the lower left, though, No. 7024 *Powis Castle,* a 1947 addition to the Class, is tooling the 9.10 a.m. from Worcester to Paddington at a slightly higher speed than optimum over the troughs – the making of spray can be seen. It is pleasant to note the coach in true Great Western colours, which is not a relic of pre-nationalisation but a result of the policy of the 'Decent Years' between 1955 and 1960 when several sets of Western Region stock were painted in these colours for use on expresses. Finally there is a fast fully-fitted freight whose engine, No. 6991 *Acton Burnell Hall* (a 'modified Hall' introduced by Hawkworth in 1944), is taking water on the down line. It is satisfying to know that at least three Castles (*Caerphilly*, *Pendennis*, and *Clun*) and two Halls survived the holocaust, while others are still being rescued from the huge scrapyard at Barry, Glamorgan, where several have not yet been cut up. These may be seen in museums or actually in steam on open days at Tyseley Shed, near Birmingham, or on Great Western Society occasions.

Willesden   Pl. 15–17

Steam, and to some extent smoke, was a characteristic part of the London scene, too. Here is a general view of the great Willesden Shed, five miles from Euston, with steam engines all over the place. Yet the photograph was taken as recently as the spring of 1964. Near though it was to Euston it was not the first Shed on the line – that was at Camden, a traditional classic roundhouse now turned into an art centre while preserving the William IV elegance of this first major engine shed in the world.

In the top picture we see the great coal hoist and coal selector which used to feed fuel into the tenders of the hundred or more engines which lived at Willesden. There are 8F Class 2–8–0 heavy freight locomotives to be seen, engines which survived to the very end of steam, and also some ubiquitous Stanier Black 5s, Britannias, and Jubilees. In this shed was housed the last working survivor of Stanier's magnificent Pacifics, *City of Nottingham*, which stood by Glasgow expresses until the end of 1964 in case of diesel failures. Today all the steam engines are gone, and most of the diesels, too, for this is an all-electric main line using the successful overhead 25KV system.

We also see an impressive interior scene at Willesden, with a 'Black 5' on the turntable inside the roundhouse. This gives a clear idea of conditions inside a major shed, which, with shafts of sunlight and vents allowing the escape of smoke from simmering engines resting in their places, was by no means as grimy as might have been thought. But there were always smuts in the air, so that an engine-man's cap was recommended headware.

The picture on the bottom right was taken on Cup Final Day in 1964 – May 2 to be exact – when both soccer teams were from the North-West leading to a large number of special trains 'Oop for the Coop'. Stopping at Wembley and at Wembley Park on the Neasden-Marylebone line, the trains disgorged their passengers while the locomotives went on to Willesden Shed for servicing. That is why there are so many types to be seen in the picture, including No. 70050, the second 'Firth' Pacific of the Britannia Class, built as recently as 1954. Next to *Firth of Clyde*, a Class 4 2-6-0 can be discerned, built only nine years before this picture was taken, but destined to be scrapped before a third of its useful working life was completed. Other engines in the picture are Stanier Black 5s.

Honeybourne   Pl. 18-21

Honeybourne in Worcestershire is scarcely a place at all, merely a tiny village. But it was important for the railways as a major junction and a base for banking engines helping trains with the stiff climb for four miles up 1 in 100 known as 'Honeybourne Bank' which overcame the Cotswold escarpment. The Oxford-Evesham-Worcester main line crossed the Birmingham-Gloucester line almost at right angles here, but few trains stopped at the station. Today it is still a junction but closed to the public with two of its four tracks torn up and its once attractive adornments rusting and decayed.

Climbing hard up the bank towards the Campden Tunnel in the London direction is a heavy freight train headed by No. 3809, a Consolidation Class 2-8-0 built by Collett at Swindon in 1939 (but a direct descendant of the Churchward design of 1903 – a few of which still survived at the time this picture was taken in early summer, 1964). Below we see the freight banked by a sturdy, handsome Collett 0-6-0, No. 2259. Both engines are working hard in these pictures but it was a warm day so very little steam can be seen.

In plate 20 another Collett 0-6-0, No. 2253, is seen at Honey-bourne, awaiting banking duties. These engines were introduced in 1930 and had a tractive effort of just over 20,000 lb, making them ideal for light freight trains or for banking duties. The last type of locomotive built for Britain's steam railways, a massive 9F 2–10–0, can be seen simmering in the background. Built between 1958 and 1960 (*Evening Star* of this Class, completed in the spring of 1960, was the very last standard-gauge engine built for B.R.) these engines could handle up to 800 tons on Honeybourne Bank without assistance. We see another 2–8–0 Consolidation in plate 21 taking a fully-fitted freight up to Campden on its own.

East Wales   Pl. 22, 23

Not so many years ago there was a line through the hills of East Wales between Welshpool and Oswestry. It was part of the Cambrian system which allowed through running between Chester and the Cambrian Coast at Aberystwyth and avoided Shrewsbury. Naturally it had no hope of survival when the Beeching axe started to fall. But here we have a scene before its eclipse, showing a fairly modern British Railways-built Class 5, No. 75009, hauling a passenger semi-fast northwards from Welshpool close to the small country station of Buttington. This photograph was taken on a cool bright day in April 1963, while the picture below it is three weeks later, showing a pick-up freight on the single line nearing Welshpool. The engine is No. 46519, an Ivatt taper-boilered 2–6–0 built in 1947.

Exeter   Pl. 24–26

Exeter Central was the Southern Railway's station in the Devon County Town, a proud junction where its expresses from Waterloo coming via Salisbury split up to serve the various holiday resorts of Devon and Cornwall. Greatest and most popular of these trains was the 'Atlantic Coast Express', which left Waterloo at 11 a.m. and covered the $171\frac{1}{2}$ miles to Exeter in three hours with two stops. It was the Southern's fastest train (the $83\frac{3}{4}$ miles from London to Salisbury took 80 minutes with a train of at least 12 heavy coaches) and it was the most 'multiple' train ever scheduled. It was known as the 'ACE' and carried portions for Sidmouth, Ilfracombe, Bude, Padstow, Torrington and Plymouth. Its doom was foretold in 1963 and it came to an end in 1965, but in the last three years of its life, still steam-hauled, it gave a faster run to London from Exeter than the Western Region could manage with diesel-hauled trains from Exeter St Davids to Paddington.

Here we see Merchant Navy Pacific No. 35014, *Nederland Line*, with the 'Atlantic Coast Express' headboard after arrival at Exeter on 11 June 1963. Taking over at Salisbury, this engine took its 12-coach express down Sherborne Dip in Dorset at 99 m.p.h. This I know because I was in the restaurant car at the time and had my stopwatch going. Anyway, speeds in the upper nineties were not exceptional with Merchant Navies on this train, and there were one or two authenticated hundreds in the last year of running. Even in 1967, in their final summer of action on the Southampton line, many official and unofficial recordings showed them 'topping the ton'.

Exeter Shed kept its stud of engines in excellent condition right up to the end, partly because of interest and loyalty to 'Southern Steam' and partly because in that part of the West Country they were still able to attract cleaners, the supply of labour not being so restricted as in London and other parts of the system. So we see No. 35004, *Cunard White Star*, a Merchant Navy Pacific, shining in the sun and in resplendent condition. She is probably waiting to take over the various parts of an afternoon up express to Waterloo from Plymouth and Ilfracombe. On the left is the Exmouth branch train, in the charge of a Class 4 2-6-4 tank, a standard British Railways design encountered all over the country during the last decade of steam. The Exmouth branch is still open, but worked by diesel multiple units. The extensions to once popular resorts such as Budleigh Salterton have been closed. Even the Waterloo-Exeter line is in constant danger of closure, and works on a restricted basis with Western Region diesels. In fact, the Western Region had already taken over all workings west of Salisbury at the time (June 1963) that these photographs were taken, but in the first few months there were no apparent changes from the Southern days – possibly because in the year that followed the terribly severe winter of 1962-63 the Southern Region steam-operated services in the hard-hit Devon and Cornwall area got through where Western Region's diesels had failed miserably. The locals started calling S.R. 'Steam Reliability'.

Plate 26 shows a streamlined West Country Class light Pacific, built by Bulleid in 1945, in her original condition with the designer's special valve gear. In exemplary condition externally, too, she takes water viewed from the windows of the up 'Atlantic Coast Express'. Further away a Southern 'Mogul' of the U1 Class can be seen simmering gently in the afternoon sunshine. Sometimes these Moguls took over the Plymouth section of expresses from Waterloo and hauled them round the northern part of Dartmoor for 60 miles to the city beside the Tamar. In pre-war days Exeter Central was Queen Street.

Haresfield (Winter)   Pl. 27–30

It took a bright cold winter's day to bring out the most photogenic qualities of a steam locomotive in action, for then the steam whirled white and puffy in the chill air. Watchers could envy the men on the footplate with their huge roaring fire. Here we see some wintry railway scenes at this fascinating West Country station and its environs, where the double tracks of the former Midland Railway main line from Birmingham to Gloucester and Bristol ran beside – but did not link with – those of the former Great Western Railway heading in the other general direction from Gloucester to Swindon. It was a complicated piece of permanent way for the layman, and must have been more so back in the days before the 1923 grouping, but it was a marvellous place to 'watch the trains go by'. It stayed like that until the end of 1964, and these pictures were taken in February of that last year of pure steam operation over both lines.

The picture at top left shows one of the delightful little 0–4–2 tanks of the Great Western Railway, No. 1444, dating only from 1932 despite her veteran appearance, coming along past Haresfield and its level crossing with a push-and-pull train down the ex-G.W.R. main line to Chalford, the station before Kemble. This was quite a frequent service of local push-and-pulls, serving all the tiny halts like Ebley Crossing Halt, Downfield Crossing Halt, Cashes Green Halt and Ham Mill Halt. The run was 16 miles exactly and it took about 43 minutes. Although the line remains open, all the little stations and the local service have, naturally, fallen victim to the Beeching – and post-Beeching – butchery. Not quite all the 0–4–2 tanks are lost to us, though; private owners have bought them and two may be seen in action on the lovely Dart Valley Railway between Totnes and Ashburton. In the picture the ex-Midland metals can be seen on the left, the up-and-down tracks in opposite directions to the Great Western. The push-and-pull train has come from Gloucester Central but it won't be stopping at Haresfield for this was a Midland-only station.

In the picture below we see a Midland train which, although photographed in 1964, might just as easily have been in 1924, for the engine is pure Midland. This is an up freight approaching Haresfield from the Bristol direction, and it has $5\frac{3}{4}$ miles to go to reach

Gloucester (not Central but Eastgate Station, the Midland one). This Fowler 0-6-0, No. 44605, was the very last of a huge class of 580 engines introduced between 1922 and 1925, built to a Midland design by Deeley and modified by Fowler. More than 300 of them survived to the last days of steam and most had many years of sturdy service left in them when they were wantonly destroyed.

Plate 30 shows No. 44605 passing, going well on her way towards Gloucester, her 24,500 lb of tractive effort being effectively exerted to move the heavy freight speedily and reliably through the cold winter's day.

Above it is another of the former Great Western 0-4-2 tanks, No. 1474, running light at Haresfield. She is, rather curiously, on the Midland up line and not her own metals, and in the chill air she leaks steam. There were still 24 engines of this class in existence when this picture was taken early in 1964, and there were still a few 'glories' in store for them. When the Western Region took over the Southern from Salisbury to Exeter and beyond, many branches were closed, notably those to Lyme Regis and Seaton, but a few had to remain open, such as the Yeovil Junction to Yeovil, and the Exeter to Exmouth. The Western imposed its will fairly quickly on the ex-Southern motive power, replacing modern tanks on the Exmouth branch with diesel multiple units; but for the bare two miles from Yeovil Junction (a section it was intended to close as soon as procedures could be forced through), the quite modern Southern tanks were sent away and replaced with Western Region 0-4-2s. The inaugural branch train in charge of a tiny 0-4-2 tank was much photographed by the Press at the time.

Haresfield (Summer)   Pl. 31–34

Fascinating though it was to watch trains on cold clear days at this West Country vantage point, when each passing engine was a steamy spectacular, a warm summer's day brought out all the pleasures of the true English countryside. The hedgerows and the gentle twittering life in them, the wild flowers that always gather in the grasses beside railway lines and on embankments, the stillness that settled over the scene, broken only predictably when a train was coming and not disturbed every few seconds by some unscheduled roaring lorry or snarling sports car. There were few road noises near the tracks at Haresfield.

Plate 31 shows an express train coming at speed, a Bristol-Birmingham-Derby express heading for Gloucester on the Midland up-line. It thunders into view, disturbing (and surely in a rather pleasant way) the quiet of the countryside for only half a minute and in so doing it moves hundreds of people past the watcher beside the tracks, carrying as many people as would be rushed along a road by seven dozen motor cars. An original Stanier 'Black 5' 4-6-0, No. 44666, dating from the introduction of the class in 1935, heads the train on a July day in 1963.

In plate 32 we see a Birmingham-Bristol express on the down main (ex-Midland) line, going well with a high-stepping Class 5 of fairly recent manufacture. This is No. 73015, an early member of a class designed at Doncaster and introduced in 1951, and the date of the picture is June 1963.

Another up train is shown in plate 33, in the charge of a Stanier Black 5, No. 44813, built early in 1937. This semi-fast to Gloucester and Birmingham has a very distinctive London, Midland & Scottish Railway appearance – not only is the engine pure L.M.S. from its prime but the first coach is contemporary with the locomotive, one of a great many built at Wolverton for use all over the company's widespread system. Like the Stanier Black 5s, these coaches could be found anywhere from Bournemouth West to Wick in the far north of Scotland, or from Leicester to Holyhead. This was efficient standardisation but it never degenerated, nor was it intended to, into a grey monotony of sameness. There was immense variety on the L.M.S. to the very end. Here at Haresfield in the summer of 1963, some of that variety was still to be seen. Late in July, about a month after the picture of 44813 was taken, a former Great Western Grange 4-6-0, No. 6831 *Bearley Grange,* can be seen passing the same spot but on the G.W.R. up line heading for Stroud (plate 34). The Grange Class were a mixed-traffic variation of the Halls, built from 1936 onwards, but incorporating parts of an early 2-6-0 type. In the '30s the Great Western resorted to this kind of economy with much success.

Shipton   Pl. 35, 36

On the edge of the Cotswolds, Shipton was a country station of typical Great Western design, situated on the Oxford-Evesham-Worcester main line. The line remains but the station has

142

faded into the past, along with its neighbour Ascott-under-Wychwood. It was at Shipton where, once, you alighted for Burford, one of the prettiest villages in the region. But even in the spring of 1964, when the pictures at the top of these two pages were taken, few trains stopped there. Here we see the 12.55 p.m. express from Worcester to Paddington, with restaurant cars, thundering along the up line towards its next stop at Oxford, where it was due at 2.11 p.m. The engine is No. 7025 *Sudeley Castle,* one of the later batch of Castles built by the Great Western at Swindon in 1946/47. As the train approaches (in the second picture) we can see the yellow band painted along the top of the first carriage. This indicates first class accommodation, a feature we take for granted throughout Europe these days, but in 1964 it was new on the Western Region of British Railways, and some passengers mistook it for the restaurant car.

Sudbury Hill   Pl. 37, 38

A rare visitor to the London area and even rarer at this small suburban station on the Great Central and Great Western Joint Line is a big British Railways Britannia Class locomotive at the head of a heavy passenger train. In fact the occasion was probably unique on a line which was not built until the turn of the century and knew only Great Central and Great Western engines, and latterly London and North Eastern and a few London Midland and Scottish express steam locomotives. Certainly it will never happen again, for the Britannias, like all British steam, have gone, although one or two are privately preserved. The occasion that brings 70050, *Firth of Clyde,* second of the six 'Firth' Sub-division of the Britannias intended for the Scottish Region, through the Harrow area is the Soccer Cup Final at Wembley. In 1964 both teams were from the North, on London Midland Region metals, and twelve specials made their way to Wembley, six of them using Wembley Hill station on the Marylebone line. The well-filled special makes her way slowly through Sudbury Hill with only $2\frac{1}{4}$ miles to go to reach her destination, and she has had to thread her path amid already ubiquitous diesel multiple units.

Llanbrynmair   Pl. 39–42

Here are four pictures of one train at a flag stop amid the Welsh hills. Llanbrynmair served a tiny farming community in remote country between Welshpool and Machynlleth on the old Cambrian Railway. The line passed into Great Western ownership in 1923 but that great and historic system had hardly time enough to put its characteristic stamp upon it before nationalisation came in 1948. However, it is a Great Western engine we see here, heading the 'Cambrian Coast Express'. It is a lightweight 4–6–0 of the Manor Class, built for secondary lines by Collett in 1938, and in keeping with G.W.R. economy drives in the '30s, parts of withdrawn 2–6–0s dating from 1911 were incorporated. Here, No. 7803, *Barcote Manor*, pulls slowly into the little station and stops; this was an infrequent occurrence, for Llanbrynmair was a flag stop at which the 'Cambrian Coast Express' would only call if someone was waiting to travel to points beyond Shrewsbury. The station master dealt with the signals which stopped the train.

It is 11.45 on a chilly February morning in 1965, when steam still reigned on the Welsh marches. The handsome Manor makes plenty of steam as she pulls away from her unexpected stop and heads for her next stop at Moat Lane Junction, 12 miles away. The Manor would stay in charge of her train as far as Shrewsbury, 48 miles to the east, where, in 1965, a diesel would take over the express for the run to London. Today the 'Cambrian Coast Express' is no more, replaced by diesel multiple units which are somewhat uncomfortable vehicles to ride in for so long a trip as the 83 miles from Shrewsbury to Aberystwyth. The whole section has been transferred, too, from Western Region to London Midland Region, and through trains no longer run from Paddington to Shrewsbury, the service having been shifted to Euston via the electrified line through Wolverhampton.

Vauxhall   Pl. 43, 44

A mile out of Waterloo on an August day in 1962 one could still see and admire the delightful Drummond M7 Class 0 4–4 tanks at work. They had handled empty stock workings between Waterloo and Clapham Junction for more than 30 years, and in plate 43 we see No. 30132, one of the originals built in 1898 on a duty turn moving the heavy 12-coach train made up for the 'Royal Wessex'. Nearly 65 years old, the neat little tank is still strong enough to canter this train along the four miles to Clapham Junction at up to 40 m.p.h. The M7s, which once hauled most of the London & South Western Railway's suburban services until electrification started in 1915, were a most numerous class which survived intact until 1959 despite one engine having over-run the buffers at Waterloo and fallen deep down into the lift shaft for the Waterloo and City underground. They had a tractive effort of all but 20,000 lb which enabled them to move remarkably heavy trains to and from the carriage sidings. At the beginning of 1961, 47 of the class were still at work.

Doomed simply by a single stroke of an accountant's pen as the ruthless tactics of modernisation built up, the class was condemned and replaced at once with pannier tanks from the Western Region in August and September, 1962. We see one of these, No. 3633, in plate 44. Pleasant and effective enough on their own region, working to and from Paddington, they were out of place at Waterloo and the enginemen hated the 'foreign imports'. One managed to appear in the famous Cuneo painting of Clapham Junction, but in general, they only did a year's unpopular service on the empty stock work. The picture shows 3633, built in 1933 and 35 years younger than the engine above, wearing the Western Region number she was never to change and taking the empty stock of a Holland America Line boat train from Waterloo to Clapham.

Waterloo   Pl. 45, 46

The last London terminal to hear the roar of the diesel, Waterloo held steam for main line and stock movements until July 1967. In its latter years it became a favourite gathering spot for railway enthusiasts, and its excellent Surrey Room restaurant was the venue for lunches galore, people looking out of the windows at the pleasant steamy scene. Plate 45 shows a third class of tank engine employed to haul the empty stock. This is one of British Railways' 2–6–4 tanks, a later member of a class designed at Brighton in 1951 and introduced gradually during the early '50s. Also at Waterloo were some 'Mickey Mouse' tanks, 2–6–2s designed at Swindon a year or so later, which were never popular and never very successful. These tanks had been brought in late in 1963 to take over from the ex-G.W.R. panniers, and they continued to work the empty stock until July 1967, when diesel shunters and bigger diesel units made their appearance. All these changes added considerably to British Railways' losses at this period, and the kindest thing one can say about the management at that time was that it had lost all trace of common sense. A straight handover from the M7s to diesels would have saved nearly half a million pounds, just on this short and simple stretch of line. In the picture, No. 80137 is seen at Waterloo in March 1964.

Below is a general view of Waterloo in the autumn of 1963, presenting a picture of steam power which at that time no other London terminal could offer, although there was still steam at Euston, Paddington and Marylebone. No. 35012, *United States Lines,* a Merchant Navy Pacific, stands at the head of a train for the West Country, and a Battle of Britain Pacific, No. 34077, *603 Squadron,* waits to take out a Southampton, Bournemouth and Weymouth express. Further over is an unidentified West Country Pacific, about to run 'light engine' to nearby Nine Elms shed. A Portsmouth electric express, the stock dating from the 1938 electrification of that line, is leaving from the far side. No diesels polluted the huge Waterloo roof in those days, and none in fact did so for two more years.

Waterloo and Clapham Junction   Pl. 47-49

Here is another view of Waterloo, a distant one taken in September 1963, showing four of Bulleid's Pacifics. The nearer locomotive is West Country Class No. 34017, *Ilfracombe,* two others are Merchant Navy Pacifics, and the last is another West Country.

The centre picture shows that most beautiful of all post-war express trains, the elegant 'Bournemouth Belle'. This superb Pullman train, made up daily with 12 of the best Pullmans, left Waterloo at 12.30 p.m. for a two-hour run to Bournemouth stopping at Southampton on the way. The $79\frac{3}{4}$ miles to Southampton were scheduled to take 87 minutes. Returning, the 'Belle' left Bournemouth at 4.40 p.m. It became recognised as one of the best restaurants in the South of England for lunch, and thousands enjoyed the cuisine and vintage wines served in a plush atmosphere of lincruster and moquette by skilled waiters who had been more than 20 years with the Pullman Company. The first class Pullmans, adorned with girls' names instead of numbers, boasted private coupés and compartments in addition to the main open-plan armchairs at tables. In these, meals could be served which had been ordered the day before from selected menus. It was by no means unknown for small groups of people to make the round trip to Bournemouth in order to enjoy a gastronomic lunch. On the way back, tea was served, complete with toasted tea cakes, toast, sandwiches, cakes and currant bread, a lavish and typical tea reminiscent of the best of English country houses in days gone by. The 'Belle' was doomed once the iconoclasts took over the railways, for it was too far above their appreciation to maintain. However, it survived until the end of December 1966, and even for a few months in 1967 but then it was cut down in size and hauled by a borrowed diesel which failed eight times.

Our picture shows the Merchant Navy Pacific rostered for the heavy duty (12 Pullmans and a brake van – here an ex-G.W.R. vehicle – weigh substantially more than a dozen ordinary corridor coaches) taking the 'Bournemouth Belle' through Clapham Junction at the maximum allowed speed at that busy junction of 40 m.p.h. She is No. 35005 *Canadian Pacific*, in beautiful condition. The date is 14 May 1964.

The other great train out of Waterloo was the 'Atlantic Coast Express' (see Pl. 24–26) and at the bottom of the page we see the 'ACE' hauled by Merchant Navy No. 35030, *Elder Dempster Lines*, passing Clapham Junction in September 1963. The engine is carrying the neat headboard as was the custom when railways were still proud of their equipment.

Clapham Junction Pl. 50–53

When a British journalist, overwhelmed with the massive, busy appearance of Milan station, suggested to the Station Master there that it must be the busiest in the world, that official pulled out a reference book in Italian and said – 'No, no zee beesiest – 'e is Clap-ham Yunkshon near London'. Since the journalist came from Clapham he was stunned. But this fact has been known widely for decades; Clapham Junction passes 2,400 trains a day, 100 an hour on average, but at rush hours there are three trains going through every minute. Since August 1967, no steam engines have been seen there, but up to July of that year they were still hauling the main-line expresses and a few tanks were moving empty stock, while London's 'unknown' line – the Clapham to Kensington Olympia cross-town route run mainly for postal workers with a morning and evening local – was steam-hauled until the end of August.

The views on these two pages were taken in 1963 and 1964 when steam in action was part and parcel of life at the busy junction. We see No. 82022, a 'Mickey Mouse' 2-6-2 Class 3 tank dating from

1953 (built at Swindon but far removed from Great Western designs) moving empty stock towards the automatic carriage washing plant. In plate 51 an up parcels train comes cantering through at the maximum allowed speed of 40 m.p.h. hauled by West Country Pacific No. 34031, *Torrington*.

Plate 52 shows a semi-fast train from Southampton pulling away from a signal check on its final run of four miles to Waterloo. It is hauled by one of the latest class of Black 5s introduced, the high-stepping 73000s. Twenty of these, after allocation to the Southern Region following the withdrawal in 1961–62 of the King Arthur Class, received names perpetuating those much loved engines. They became known as the 'fake Arthurs', and this one is 73119, *Elaine*. Some enthusiasts thought this naming of steam engines as late as 1962 a warm-hearted gesture by the Southern Region and responded to it. Others felt it was an insult to their beloved 'Arthurs'. But these new Class 5s were speedy engines and put up performances worthy of their predecessors. The whole idea seems to have merited a credit mark on the part of Southern management in the early '60s – a management which did in fact use its steam power intelligently and for a much longer period than other British systems. It could never be said that the original 'King Arthurs' were retired ahead of their time – most of them served 35 years and more. But the new Class 5s had a very short innings and their wholesale destruction in 1967 was absurd. Electrification of the main line to Southampton and Bourne-mouth eliminated any need for them on this run but they could and should have worked to Salisbury and the West where they would have been far better and more reliable than the borrowed 'Warship' diesels from the Western Region.

Plate 53 shows the *Queen Mary* boat train entering Clapham Junction from Waterloo in 1965. The streamlined Bulleid Battle of Britain Class Pacific No. 34083, *605 Squadron*, carries the 'Cunarder' headboard and denotes that it is the first section, intended for first class passengers. Cabin and Tourist passengers for the great ship will already have gone down to Southampton in an earlier train carrying both first and second class carriages. It happens that I was aboard this particular boat train, and the filthy condition of the handsome engine caused an American to comment – on seeing it at the dockside when the train had run alongside the *Queen Mary* – that if any American railroad had allowed an engine to get so dirty the general manager would have been fired. I replied that he would have been on the Southern, too, in the days before nationalisation. . . .

Woodford Halse

Pl. 54, 55

The Great Central Railway came late to London, forcing an expensive path to town from Rugby to a new terminus at Marylebone, at the turn of the century. Though magnificently run, the new line was never a financial success, and it slowly worsened over the years, through London and North Eastern days to the time of the State system. Once the Beeching era had begun, it seemed likely the old Great Central was doomed, and the line was allowed to run down. In 1964 the position was grim, with just a few semi-fast passenger trains from Marylebone to Leicester and Nottingham and some freight services.

Woodford Halse was a pleasant country station, the junction for an 11-mile branch to Banbury, situated 69 miles from Marylebone. Most trains which still survived on the former Great Central in the '60s called there, and a number of the outer-outer-suburban services terminated there. Because of the run-down, no diesels worked on the line except for fast freight trains, and so various classes of locomotive saw out their days between Marylebone and Nottingham. Here we see, in plate 54, one of Sir Nigel Gresley's famous V1 Green Arrow Class, No. 60828, running slowly as a light engine through Woodford Halse. She cannot long have been assigned to former Great Central metals, for there are few signs of neglect and she is clean and green, reminiscent of the condition of these engines in L.N.E.R. days.

At the foot of the page a big 9F Class 2–10–0 in filthy state stands around simmering at Woodford Halse on a Saturday in May 1964, probably waiting to take over a freight coming from Banbury. It seems incredible that these big engines, the latest and largest standard class designed by British Railways, should be wasted and allowed to degenerate into this sort of condition. The last three members of the class were built at Swindon after B.O.A.C. took delivery of its Boeing 707 intercontinental jet aircraft!

West Country

Pl. 56, 57

Deep amid the delights of rural Devon a light railway was built as recently as 1926 by the Southern Railway Company. It was the

Halwill and Torrington Light Railway, laid to standard gauge over $20\frac{1}{2}$ miles of the loveliest pastoral country in the south-west of England. Rhododendrons abounded on the little stations, and the single line ran through deep cuttings covered in flowers or through rolling fields with scarcely a trace of human habitation. It was this absence of humans in the hard atmosphere of the '60s which killed the line – that and a drop in light freight traffic in clay and coal. There were only two trains a day in each direction, with a third running part of the way from Torrington, just to Dunsbear Halt, $5\frac{1}{2}$ miles.

Halwill was quite a junction in its way, with one line going to Padstow, another to Bude, a third to Okehampton and Exeter, while the 'new' light railway curved away to the north. It was the beginning of the lines known as the 'withered arm' of the old London and South Western Railway, a region which never produced profitable traffic but was accepted cheerfully by the company which subsidised it from its more lucrative routes. This was the sort of situation which benefitted the travelling public in the days when the railways were owned by the people as shareholders.

The motive power used on the line was strikingly modern considering its remote location. In 1961 the 'Mickey Mouse' 2-6-2 tanks allocated to Southern Region (and built between 1952 and 1955) came to North Devon to work the Halwill and Torrington. Here we see one taking water at Hatherleigh Station in June 1963, as it pauses half way along the light railway while hauling a two-coach train (plus some parcels and goods wagons) to Torrington. In the lower picture the engine stands at Petrockstow station on the same June day, on a single line flanked by glorious displays of rhododendrons.

Today the light railway runs only to Petrockstow and Meeth Halt for occasional clay or passenger traffic and, worse still, even Torrington has lost its rail link with Barnstaple Junction.

Fleet   Pl. 58–63

During the last days of steam on the Southern the Hampshire town of Fleet on the four-track main line from Basingstoke to Waterloo was much visited by railway enthusiasts. They were treated to the frequent sight of express trains hurtling through at maximum speed, a situation which lasted until July 1967. Since electrification,

Fleet has changed from a country town to a commuter dormitory where new housing estates have sprung up fostered by an electric service to Waterloo running every half-hour and taking 47 minutes for the $36\frac{1}{2}$ miles.

From an attractive lineside vantage point on a quiet road once used for military training, superb views could be obtained, and on summer days many people picnicked there to watch the trains go by. Here are some shots taken from that location in the summers of 1963 and 1964, before the laying of the third rail which spelled doom for steam.

At top left, modified West Country Pacific No. 34017, *Ilfracombe*, in very clean condition heads a Bournemouth express at 70 m.p.h. on the down fast line. Plate 59 shows the beautiful 'Bournemouth Belle' at 75 m.p.h. in the charge of Merchant Navy Pacific No. 35014, *Nederland Line*. The bottom picture presents another Merchant Navy, No. 35002 *Union Castle Line*, on the down 'Royal Wessex', an express which left Waterloo at 4.35 p.m. and made the run to Winchester (66 miles) in 65 minutes. This view is taken from the bridge across the tracks a mile on the London side of Fleet and shows the remains of Pyeshott Camp platform, built during the War to serve a large army establishment based in the heathland abounding on the Surrey-Hants border.

Plate 61 is of a local stopping train, typical of the somewhat infrequent services which in steam days kept this a countrified area. No. 34097, *Holsworthy*, a modified West Country Pacific, is gathering speed in the up direction after a stop at Fleet. She is hauling a train of varied stock, the first two coaches being former London Midland Region non-corridor suburban carriages transferred from the Southend line after electrification.

Plate 62 shows the up 'Bournemouth Belle' at more than 80 m.p.h. – a speed commonly achieved or even exceeded on the long straight gentle downgrade between Basingstoke and Woking. The engine is Merchant Navy Class Pacific No. 35019, *French Line C.G.T.*, and her 500-ton luxury load is being hustled from Bournemouth Central to Waterloo in two hours.

Fastest moving of all the Fleet pictures is the shot of a 73000 Clas 5, a 'fake Arthur', hurtling up from Southampton to Waterloo on Saturday, 13 July 1963, whipping through Fleet at fully 90 m.p.h. Grime and speed prevented the number and nameplate being read.

Abergavenny   Pl. 64–67

Late autumn on the Welsh border as the 1960s advanced into the
middle of the decade presented a rather tired but still varied railway
scene. Steam continued to dominate the hilly main line between
Abergavenny in Monmouthshire and Hereford, but it had only a year
to go. In plate 64 we see a former Great Western 'Hall', No. 6918,
Sandon Hall, in an appalling condition on a train coming in from the
Newport direction. One of more than 200 Halls built for mixed traffic
by Collett, this engine's filthy state would never have been tolerated
by Great Western management. Like the once ubiquitous Halls, the
water tank seen at the end of the platform has disappeared from the
railway scene as steam is no longer in action.

The long climb into the fringes of the Brecon Mountains and the
hills of West Hereford called for bankers on heavy freight trains.
Plate 65 shows an unusual 2–8–2 Tank engine with extended bunker
and trailing wheels, a Collett rebuild of Churchward's 4200 Class of
2–8–0 tanks. The tank, simmering at Abergavenny and waiting for
duty, dates back to 1934 but the Class design was introduced in 1910.

A great deal of devoted work went into the shaping of station roofs
and friezes, each company in the old days having distinctive designs.
In plate 66 the neat friezes of Abergavenny station are featured, with
a distant view of a train with banker climbing up towards Hereford.
At the bottom of the page is a Pannier tank, 0–6–0 No. 3708,
acting as station pilot and assistant banker. Her condition is sympto-
matic of the sloth which overtook sheds (with the apparent acceptance of management). This tank, built in 1933, is so dirty that her
number has been chalked on the rear of the bunker.

Winter   Pl. 68–71

Winter is a time when railways, and steam railways especially, play
a bigger part in transport. This is when cars won't start, or get stuck
in snow, when aircraft are delayed by fog or diverted because of
cross-winds and sleet. To the observer of steam in action, there was
the dramatic plume of steam and smoke, heightened and widened by
chilly air, and the comforting glow of the furnace at night. Steam
engines gave off a warmth as you moved near them, and the familiar,
nostalgic smell was intensified. In bitter conditions, steam engines
were just as reliable as in summer, and when it came to snow and
frost their sheer strength carried them through all but the worst

drifts. Many were the occasions when steam engines had to be brought out to haul third-rail electrics on the Southern Railway. Floodwater, too, could be traversed by large-wheeled locomotives, up to and beyond depths which swamped the works of diesels.

Some wintry sights are recalled on these pages. In plate 68 the 'Atlantic Coast Express', up from Exeter, pauses at Salisbury before the final non-stop run to Waterloo. The engine, Merchant Navy No. 35001, *Channel Packet,* first of the class dating from 1941, is seen during coal-trimming operations early in 1963. Although in her 22nd year, the driver said that she felt – and ran – as if she were a two-year-old.

Below the Salisbury picture is a February scene dating from 1964 showing a former Great Western Railway 2–8–2 tank No. 7206 (1934 vintage) climbing, bunker first, between Crumlin and Pontypool in Monmouthshire, making a lot of steam as she tackles the gradient.

Another steamy scene in cold weather is seen in plate 70, where we see a former Great Western 'Prairie' tank heading a local passenger train from Gloucester to Ross-on-Wye on a track now obliterated under the Beeching axe. No. 4107, a 2–6–2 tank introduced in 1929, is between Blaisdon and Longhope in 1964. At least two of these 'Prairie' tanks survive in private ownership, but as to Blaisdon and Longhope, they have passed into the limbo of forgotten places.

Plate 71 takes a look across the Scottish border, at Perth early in 1965. An express for Glasgow leaves in charge of a Stanier Black 5 4–6–0, No. 44767, heading into the gathering winter dusk. This line, and the Aberdeen via Forfar route, remained steam-operated until quite late in 1966, after early and disastrous experiences with diesels in the late fifties. Many sound express engines were based at Perth Shed until the end of 1966, a length of survival exceeded only by the Southern Region's Southampton and Salisbury lines and the Leeds-Stockport-Barrow triangle.

Gloucester   Pl. 72–75

Until quite recently the cathedral city of Gloucester was a railway centre of consequence, with two stations and two engine sheds. Enthusiasts could spend many happy hours here, and even those whose interest in railways was confined to the appreciative glance at a steam engine took for granted the presence in such a place as

Gloucester Midland Region station of several friendly simmering engines. Such a steamy scene presents itself in December 1963 when the general view of Gloucester Eastgate was taken. Locomotives can be seen making their distinctive marks upon the landscape and the one in action is a nearly new 9F Class 2-10-0, No. 92000, waiting with a freight train. Plate 74 gives another view of Eastgate, taken in March 1963, with up to 15 locomotives visible outside the great Shed. A former Great Western 'Castle' stands near the signal gantry, and an ex-Midland 0-6-0 is on the right of the picture.

Lower left is a shot of a former London Midland and Scottish Jubilee Class express engine, No. 45685 *Barfleur,* heading a train for Cheltenham and the North. The Jubilees, one of the most elegant classes ever designed, totalled nearly 200 engines, and were introduced in 1934 as a Stanier taper-boiler development of the 'Patriots' built by Fowler. Three of them survive in private ownership today. In this picture it is interesting to note the ex-L.N.E.R. parcels and mail coach directly behind the tender. The date is July 1963.

The last of the four Gloucester pictures, plate 75, shows Gloucester Central, the Western Region station, on 11 May 1964. Starting away with an express freight is former G.W.R. No. 6845, *Paviland Grange,* and an 0-4-2 push-and-pull tank, No. 1444, waits in the background.

Trelewis   Pl. 76, 77

Deep amid the Welsh Valleys there used to be a branch line running from Nelson to Dowlais, $9\frac{1}{2}$ miles long. Not only is it now gone, but so is the 'main line' off which it sprang – the Pontypool Road to Aberdare route. But on 12 May 1964 it was very much in action, and the first station out from Nelson was Trelewis Platform, a tiny place which served a few colliery people and railwaymen. Here an 0-6-2 tank specially built by Collett for service in the Welsh valleys, No. 5605, with an elongated boiler and dating from 1927, stops to set down a railwayman passenger who had been riding on the engine up from Nelson. The train is the 3.25 p.m. from Nelson, a workman's service with very low fares which ran through to a place called Ystrad Mynach. The lower picture shows the train getting under way on a line already dying, for only one track is in regular use, and a year later neither was functioning.

Crumlin   Pl. 78, 79

One of the most dramatic viaducts ever to put trains in the landscape was the graceful structure at Crumlin in South Wales. It swept high above the valley of the Ebbw River, the rails carried 193 feet above the water on ten spans each 150 feet long. There was an intervening hill, but seven spans were on the Pontypool side and three on the Crumlin town side. This bold construction was completed in May 1857 at the negligible cost (even for those days) of £62,000. Thomas Kennard designed it and the ironwork was made at Blaenavon but pre-fabricated (this process is more than a century old, notwithstanding the fuss modern public relations people make about it) in a foundry on the site. Altogether, 1,300 tons of wrought iron, 1,250 tons of cast iron, 800 cubic yards of masonry, and 25,000 cubic yards of timber went into its construction. The first piece was laid by Lady Isabella Fitzmaurice at the Isabella Pier on 8 December 1853, and it is said that a casket of new coins was buried under it. But when the iconoclasts came along to close the line and destroy a great work which had stood for 109 years – carrying millions of tons of traffic – they found no treasure. They did, however, sell the scrap metal for a price a good deal higher than was paid for the entire viaduct in early Victorian days. Shortly before destruction, the Crumlin Viaduct was used as the set for the climactic moments of a film starring Sophia Loren and Gregory Peck; but this was its last fling, for after being a dominant feature of the skyline for so long it came down in April 1966.

In plate 78 we see a former Great Western pannier tank hauling a local passenger train gently across the viaduct towards Crumlin High Level. The train was going from Pontypool Road to Aberdare.

Plate 79 shows a broad view of the graceful viaduct over the Ebbw Vale, and on it is the 11.52 train from Crumlin High Level to Pontypool Road photographed on 12 May 1964. All local passenger trains were in the hands of 0–6–0 pannier tanks from the end of the war, but heavier engines, like the 'Aberdare' Moguls, worked coal traffic.

Barnstaple   Pl. 80–87

Barnstaple Junction was one of the last major junctions in the West Country to retain the atmosphere and action of steam operations. At all times of the day and night engines were in motion, moving in and out of the local shed, taking trains on to the various branches, or standing in steam ready to accept duties. Barnstaple is not such a large town but it became a railway centre by stages, latterly receiving a line from Exeter (Southern Region) and a line from Taunton (Western Region), while it sent off a line to the popular holiday resort of Ilfracombe and another to Bideford and Torrington (jointly worked by Western and Southern engines but owned by the Southern Railway in earlier days before passing to the Southern Region and then the Western).

Today all life is gone from Barnstaple, and it has degenerated into a single-line terminus for passenger services by multiple-unit trains coming up – infrequently – from Exeter. Local freight services still run to Torrington but the Ilfracombe line, once heavily used in the summer months and carrying through trains from Waterloo, has been closed.

Our pictures recall it in June 1963, in the twilight of steam operation but just as busy as it always was. At top left we see a Churchward 2–6–0 of the former Great Western Railway, No. 7304, which has worked in with a semi-fast train from Taunton over the 46-mile secondary line serving lush Devon towns and villages such as Wiveliscombe and Dulverton on the way. At lower left the same train is leaving, taking the line to Torrington, $14\frac{1}{4}$ miles away. This line had only passed into Western Region management a year before but they seemed determined to put a 'G.W.R.' stamp upon it during the brief time it had left, and so most trains going round to Bideford and Torrington had former Great Western engines even if some rolling stock was still Southern.

Plate 81 gives a general view of Barnstaple Junction with two trains standing in the station, one for Taunton and one for Torrington. Here, an Ivatt 2–6–2 tank, built for the London Midland and Scottish in 1946 and very much a foreigner in this part of England, No. 41214, stands ready to take the Torrington train. The lower picture captures the arrival from Ilfracombe of an express for Exeter and Waterloo, headed by a Southern Battle of Britain Pacific No. 34079, *141 Squadron*, in her original streamlined casing. In plate 84 the sharp and dramatic approach from the Ilfracombe branch to Barnstaple across the bridge over the Taw River is shown. An Ilfracombe to Exeter train, hauled by Battle of Britain Pacific No. 34070, *Manston*, is about to cross the bridge, and across the page in plate 85 we see a close-up of streamlined *Manston* on the bridge.

Plates 86 and 87 give us a glimpse of an operation never likely to be seen again in Britain, not even with preserved engines. Coaling from a hoist was an essential part of a railway centre's activity and Barnstaple Junction was the only source of locomotive coal in North Devon when these pictures were taken in 1963.

A Southern 'Mogul' of the N Class, No. 31844, receives coal in her tender from the chute outside the Shed. These 2–6–0 locomotives were widely used on West Country lines as well as in Kent prior to 1961, and even at the beginning ôf 1963 there were still 80 of them at work. They were introduced by Maunsell to the South Eastern and Chatham Railway in 1917 and lasted well, giving a magnificent return on capital investment to their owners. Their reward was the scrapheap, all the class together, at the stroke of an accountant's pen (writing, some believe, under oil pressure).

Worcestershire   Pl. 88–91

'Once upon a time,' we might tell our children and our grand-children, 'when you were in the country there would often come into view a long plume of smoke.' We could say that 'it heralded one of the finest sights and sounds the world has ever known as man's first great mechanical invention thundered past on the well kept rails of England'. Perhaps too eulogistic for many people, but true just the same. At the time we tended to take sights like these a bit for granted, but fortunately Tony Hudson with his camera – out in the Worcestershire countryside – recorded some of the scenes for posterity.

Plate 88 shows a distant Castle in almost Great Western condition heading a down express to Worcester near Drake's Broughton. In the plate below, we see a typical country scene of sheep and steam and green fields in the autumn. Here is a train going north towards Birmingham, taken from a point near Oddingley on the former Midland Railway.

In plate 90 there is a superb plume of steam, trailing from a freight train going southwards towards Gloucester, also photographed near Oddingley. The lower picture on this page records the passage of a Worcester-Paddington express at speed near Stoulton (between Worcester and Evesham). Headed by No. 7004, *Eastnor Castle*, the date is five days before Christmas 1962, which was ten days before blizzards blanketed the area to mark the start of the worst winter for many years. These lines were not free of snow again until the middle of March 1963!

Cheltenham Pl. 92–94

On the same December day that the Great Western express was captured by Hudson's camera at Stoulton this former Midland Deeley-Fowler 0–6–0 goods engine hove into view on a pick-up goods entering Cheltenham. This one, No. 43979, is one of a batch introduced in 1911–12, superheated by Fowler, then Chief Mechanical Engineer of the Midland Railway.

Across the way, in plate 93, an express freight is seen leaving Cheltenham for the north, and in the same location the picture below records one of the handsome 'Jubilee' 4–6–0s, No. 45635 *Tobago*, taking an express northwards to Birmingham and Derby.

Bromsgrove Pl. 95–98

About 14 miles south of Birmingham stands the town of Bromsgrove, at the foot of the Lickey hills. It is on the busy former Midland main line from Derby to Bristol, a line which is getting busier as the years go by. But a terrible obstacle existed to prevent fast running, an obstacle just two miles long and beginning at the Bromsgrove platform end – the Lickey Incline. The gradient is 1 in 37 – nothing to a motor car, but extremely severe for a train, especially for a freight weighing 750 tons. The Incline lifts the line up through the Lickey hills to Blackwell, by which time it is on a gentle gradient on top of the Midland plain.

The Lickey Incline is the steepest railway gradient of any main line in the British Isles. For many years a special 0–10–0 banker of the Midland Railway (called 'Big Bertha') was employed to push trains up it, and all trains coming down from Blackwell had to stop dead and then proceed gradually. All goods trains had to stop and pin down the brakes of every wagon in the days before fully-fitted freights. Once London Midland, the Lickey is now part of the Western Region.

In 1969 the sharp part of the gradient at the platform end of Bromsgrove station was smoothed by raising the tracks, allowing the speed limit through the station to be raised to 75 m.p.h. In the direction of Birmingham, trains are now allowed to 'charge' the incline and a 2,500 h.p. diesel can take 250 tons over the top. If this had been possible in steam days remarkable results and splendid sounds would have been achieved.

In plate 95 a once ubiquitous Class 4 Fowler 0-6-0 No. 43979 makes an unnatural amount of smoke starting away from Bromsgrove station after taking a banker, while in plate 97 we see an unusual visitor to the Midland main line, the former Great Western Railway engine No. 5393, *Tangley Hall*. She is heading a freight train at Bromsgrove and waiting for a banker to be attached. In plate 96, two pannier tanks of the former Great Western Railway, both powerful machines despite their diminutive size, stand ready to bank a heavy train up to Blackwell on 27 August 1963. Plate 98 shows another type of banker, the largest and heaviest class employed on the Incline with the exception of the great Midland 'decapod' built specially for it fifty years ago. This is a Class 9F 2-10-0, No. 92129, built in 1955 from a Brighton design with a tractive effort of almost 40,000 lb. This picture, taken late in 1963, indicates that these engines, locally called 'track spreaders', were already out of favour and unloved. The condition of the locomotive is particularly filthy.

Lickey Pl. 99-102

Day and night the big engines thundered up the Lickey Incline, never less than one at the head and one at the rear of every train. These scenes, on the Incline itself, were during the last full summer of steam operation, 1963, and they depict action which had not changed for more than a decade, except that an even heavier and newer class of steam engine, the Class 9F 2-10-0s, had appeared as the last steam engines to be built by British Railways.

In plates 99 and 100 we see a Bristol to Birmingham passenger train headed by a fairly modern Class 5 4-6-0, No. 73068, struggling up the Lickey in August banked by a former Great Western Pannier tank. Plate 101 gives a full view of an up freight going towards Birmingham, both engines working hard. Across in plate 102 is a striking shot of two trains passing in the middle of the 1 in 37 bank, a Class 5 4-6-0 cantering down towards Bromsgrove while a 9F 2-10-0 thunders up the hill banking a freight train.

Aylesbury Pl. 103-105

The sad decline and neglect of the Great Central line from London's Marylebone terminus to Leicester, Nottingham and

Sheffield brought certain types of engine to work semi-fast trains over its tracks during the last years. While it is true to say that the Great Central came too late to London to be a really profitable railway, there was an inherited tradition of dislike towards it from other railwaymen which lasted into the 1960s. Old Midland and London and North Western men are said to have encouraged its demise.

By 1964 the expensive line was a mere shadow of its former self, with only four semi-fast trains a day to the Midlands. Some 'Royal Scots', once proud monarchs of the L.M.S., were transferred to work out their days on its inferior trains to Nottingham. Aylesbury, the main town of Buckinghamshire, 38 miles from Marylebone, was the first stop for the surviving steam semi-fasts. Today it is the end of the Great Central, the tracks torn up beyond it, and the only trains coming in are the hourly diesel multiple units from Marylebone, or a branch service every two hours from Princes Risborough.

Here is a 'Royal Scot', still showing her green colours but tired and ageing, pulling away from Aylesbury on an April day in 1964, bound for Rugby, Leicester and Nottingham. The handsome engine, No. 46163, *Civil Service Rifleman,* dating from 1928 but rebuilt by Stanier with a taper boiler with the rest of the class of 71 in 1943–44, is watched by some admiring boys at the end of the platform. Apart from Perth and Carlisle, the Great Central section was the only place left where 'Royal Scots' could be seen at work this far advanced into the twilight of steam. As the engine draws abreast and then passes into the Buckinghamshire countryside with her comparatively light train, it can be seen quite clearly that the nameplate is missing. This, together with the one on the other side, had been removed and sold to dealers, for this type of souvenir was already beginning to be valuable. British Railways at first blamed vandals for raiding sheds and stealing name plates (and this did happen on several occasions) but it transpired the authorities were doing most of the damage. Many still regret the actions of iconoclasts in dismembering a proud engine before actually withdrawing her from service, and selling the nameplates. Had B.R. waited a little longer, in fact, they would have received higher prices.

Ryde, Isle of Wight   Pl. 106–112

Once the Mecca of Victorian holidaymakers, the Isle of Wight managed to keep its charm and atmosphere right up to 1966 before surrendering to the mass motor invader. The railway system, once extensive and amazingly varied with four different companies working lines, remained intact until 1951, and survived to a large extent until 1966. The scene remained unchanged for fully 40 years with charming little Adams 02 0-4-4 tanks (33 of them) handling almost all the passenger traffic, with three tiny Stroudley 'Terrier' tanks for the Ventnor West Line and three 0-6-0 Stroudley E Class tanks dealing with the goods. Rolling stock was of Brighton and South Western vintage to the very end, displaced from the London suburbs by electrification between 1925 (South Eastern section) and 1929 (Brighton section). The engines came to the island ahead of the rolling stock, replacing the interesting little tanks of the early island companies, some of which – on the Isle of Wight Railway – lasted 45 years.

People who spent holidays on the Isle of Wight as tiny children in the early and late '20s could return to their old haunts when entering middle age and be delighted by exactly the same peaceful railway scenes. It was still quite easy, even in the summer of 1965, to cross by steam paddle-boat from Portsmouth to Ryde and board a train hauled by (quite possibly) the same engine that hauled a visitor 40 years earlier.

Then, suddenly, the spirit of modernisation, which had been held at bay for a while by the Solent and Spithead and the desire of the islanders to keep their traditions, slashed across the narrow waters and destroyed the system. Ryde to Cowes was closed in 1965, opened again for a while after a tremendous fight, but finally closed in 1966, and the Ryde to Ventnor went late in 1966. Today, there is a London underground train service running on electrified lines for eight miles from Ryde Pier Head to Shanklin, and that is all that remains of a network once comprising close on 60 miles. Big buses, too cumbersome for Isle of Wight lanes, vie with ubiquitous motor cars for road space, and more cars pour in now that drive-on ferries make it cheap and easy to cross from the mainland. Cars used to be kept down by infrequent and very costly ferries in order that the full charm of the island should be undisturbed. The effect has been to change and ruin the old character of Isle of Wight holidays, and to put little of general benefit in its place.

In the last summer of proper railway operation Tony Hudson's camera caught two delectable little Adams tanks at Ryde Pier Head station. We see them in silhouette in plate 106 on 16 August 1966 (but it could have been August 1926 if colour films had existed in those days). The picture below is in fact an earlier one, pre-dating it by three years, but the equipment is the same. Doom was not then in the air and two trains on Ryde Pier, seen from the Pierhead platform end, mean that both Ventnor and Cowes lines were in full operation. These Adams 02 Class tanks all had names awarded to them after they came to the island; they were built between 1889 and 1892, but fitted with Westinghouse brakes directly after the grouping of 1923; their transfer to the Isle of Wight took place in stages during the '20s.

Plate 108, the double-page spread, is a canvas recording for all time what Ryde Pier Head was like at holiday times. This was Whit Monday 1964, but again it could have been two or three decades earlier. Certainly it is almost exactly the same – even to the paddle steamer *Ryde* and No. 29, *Alverstone*, heading the Ventnor train – as I saw it on the last peace-time Bank Holiday, August 1939.

An over-zealous young Army officer nearly wrecked this scene for ever shortly after Dunkirk in 1940. Hearing that piers around the South Coast were to be destroyed or cut in half to foil enemy landings, he and his men planted a charge on Ryde Pier (regardless of four railway tracks and two trains at the Pier Head station) and were about to evacuate personnel when railway officials managed to detain him and hand him over to higher and more sensible authority!

The handsome paddler *Ryde* seen in this picture in her Southern Railway (later Southern Region) colours was built in 1937 together with *Sandown*. Coal burners, they had immense capacity and one was still working in 1969, pressed into service to handle the thousands attending a 'pop' festival near Ryde. The Ventnor train was always first away after the steamer from Portsmouth had disembarked her throng, and then the Cowes train followed. In this instance, though, owing to the Bank Holiday there were two trains for the Ventnor line. Services on this mainly single-track 12-mile route were so intense that Americans representing several U.S. railroads came over in pre-war days to study operations.

Plates 109–112 were all taken at Ryde Esplanade station on Whit Monday, 1964. On the left are two views of No. 30, *Shorwell,* coming off the Pier onto dry land at the Esplanade platform end, heading a Ventnor train. In plate 111 No. 14, *Fishbourne,* (the oldest 02 tank, dating from 1889) leaves the Esplanade for Cowes heading towards the tunnel under the hilly resort town, and below it we see No. 29 *Alverstone* running bunker first – as was the custom – towards the Pierhead. On the left can be seen the tracks of the Ryde Pier tramway, which for many years was a Drewry electric railcar. The paddle-steamer *Ryde* is discernible in the background.

Newport, Isle of Wight   Pl. 113–116

Capital of the island, Newport is now without a railway service but in its heyday it was justifiably called the 'Clapham Junction of the Isle of Wight'. From six in the morning to midnight there were trains in action on one or more lines, and the period from April 1945 to the beginning of 1951 saw its most intensive services. The summer service called for trains every half an hour between Cowes and Ryde via Newport, and every half an hour from Newport to Freshwater, while an hourly service went off to Sandown via Merstone Junction. In the summer of 1947 Newport was handling 76 trains a day for passengers alone, while some goods services went through it to Medina River Wharf.

These pictures were taken during 1965, the last full year of workings on the Cowes line, which was the last line to survive. Already the lines to Freshwater via Yarmouth had disappeared and the Merstone-Sandown line had rusted. In plate 113 the view is of the empty station looking towards Cowes ($4\frac{1}{2}$ miles away). Below it we are looking south, with a train from Ryde coming in over the bridge (a swing bridge rarely used as such) crossing the Medina River. The driver is about to collect his token from the linesman holding it out. On the left, No. 29, *Alverstone*, is waiting to cross the down train.

In plate 115 another view looking towards Cowes picks up a light engine, No. 21 *Sandown*, and shows some sidings which have now all disappeared into 'tatty' waste ground. The lower picture is a close-up of No. 31, *Chale*, taking water at Newport while running bunker first with an up train to Ryde.

Cowes, Isle of Wight   Pl. 117–120

Cowes was an important yachting centre in very early Victorian times, and it was not long before railways came on the scene. The Isle of Wight Central was opened between Cowes and Newport ($4\frac{1}{2}$ miles) in 1862, and the yachting centre managed to celebrate the line's centenary, but only just. By the end of 1965 it was clear that only a few months of intermittent working remained, and for years now the handsome little terminal station, once so busy and so well run, has been rotting and useless.

Trains coming in from Newport stopped first at Mill Hill, half a mile from the Cowes terminus, then ran downhill through a 208-yard tunnel which let out onto doubled track for entry into the station. In plate 117 we see a train from Ryde and Newport, having completed its $14\frac{1}{4}$-mile, 42-minute run, entering the terminus. An unusual manoeuvre then took place, whereby the engine pushed out the empty stock well beyond a cross-over, uncoupled, and crossed to the other line, still facing Cowes. The empty carriages, in charge of the guard, ran back by gravity shunt to the buffers to await the engine which came back on the train line and coupled up to run bunker first back to Ryde. It was unorthodox but simple and it worked. In plate 118 No. 31 *Chale* has just detached from her train prior to running round it. These pictures were taken late in August 1965, the last summer that Cowes enjoyed railway service.

Plate 119 shows No. 18 *Ningwood* coming into Cowes with a Sunday train from Ryde in September 1963. The neat frieze work of the station roof will be noted. Across the page is a view of the little Cowes 'suburban' station of Mill Hill with its single line platform. No. 35, *Freshwater*, running bunker first, is taking an evening train to Newport and Ryde, early in September 1964.

Wroxall, Isle of Wight   Pl. 121, 122

Situated near the top of quite a gruelling climb known as the Apse Bank (involving nearly $1\frac{1}{2}$ miles of 1 in 70) was the pleasant little country station of Wroxall, between Shanklin and Ventnor in an area of rolling hills close to St Boniface Down. Wroxall was unique in having the only refreshment room on an intermediate station in the Isle of Wight.

The Isle of Wight Railway, always a profitable enterprise, got its line open from Ryde to this point in 1866. Sadly, it missed celebrating its centenary by a year, for the line was cut short to end at Shanklin, where the converted London underground trains coming from Ryde now turn round. The sound of a gallant little Adams 02 Class tank barking its way up the Apse Bank was a delight which can, fortunately, be recalled by anyone who obtains the long-playing record 'Last Train to Ryde' produced by Eyemark in 1967.

164

On 29 June 1965, there were still trains to Ventnor and the top picture shows one from Ryde just leaving Wroxall and facing a further steep climb of 1 in 88 to the tunnel under St Boniface Down, highest point on the Isle of Wight. The lower picture was taken near the tunnel entrance and we see a Ventnor-Ryde train emerging, the Adams tank running bunker first on its way down to Wroxall.

Despite the steepness of this line and the single track, high summer used to see a train every 15 minutes on peak Saturdays, and the climb was undertaken readily by a long-lived Isle of Wight Railway locomotive, *Ryde*, built in 1864. This Beyer-Peacock 2-4-0 tank ran 1,556,846 miles before it was withdrawn in 1932, and for nine years the sturdy little engine ran in company with the bigger Adams 0-4-4 tanks.

Ventnor, Isle of Wight   Pl. 123, 124

Victorians used to winter in Ventnor, partly because the Queen in residence at Osborne House made the island fashionable, and partly because the resort really is sunny with a southern aspect protected from the north by the bulk of St Boniface Down. Today's travellers have discovered Madeira, the Canaries, Bermuda, and the West Indies, and the Edwardians went to the South of France, so Ventnor has not enjoyed a smart winter season since about the turn of the century. It no longer enjoys a railway service.

The line from Ryde was cut short at Shanklin at the end of 1965. The other line from Newport via Merstone Junction, a wonderfully scenic route, was closed in 1953. There were two stations at the resort, both terminals, a reminder of its former importance. Plates 123 and 124 show the Isle of Wight Railway terminal for trains from Ryde. The upper one is taken from a path high above the station leading to the downs, and embraces a train emerging from the tunnel (1,312 yards long) below St Boniface, on 28 September 1965.

The lower photograph reminds us how neat and well-kept Ventnor station was, even towards the end. Flower boxes were freshly prepared each day and the platforms washed and swept. Here is a scene in August 1964, with a train from Ryde nearing the end of its journey as it comes out of the tunnel. The engine is No. 18, *Ningwood*.

Weybridge   Pl. 125

Commuters on the platforms at the Surrey station of Weybridge, 19 miles from Waterloo, used to be treated to some grand sights which most of the men at any rate appreciated. Here is a typical one, on the morning of Friday, 3 May 1963, with a modified Battle of Britain Bulleid Pacific racing through on an up express from the West Country at 80 m.p.h. The engine, No. 34090, had the distinction of carrying the longest name on the Southern system, and possibly on all British Railways, with the heaviest brass name plate. It was *Sir Eustace Missenden, Southern Railway,* named after a war-time General Manager whose work in keeping the busy system going under air attack was honoured in many ways, not least this one.

Abermule   Pl. 126

A train on the single-line railway from Welshpool to the Cambrian Coast passing at Abermule the exact spot where one of the strangest disasters in British railway history occurred in 1921. It was part of the old Cambrian Railway system, and, though fully protected by Tyer's block instruments, two trains met head-on in a violent collision which resulted in the loss of 17 lives, including that of Lord Herbert Vane-Tempest, a Director of the Cambrian. There has never been such a collision since, but the impossible happened on that occasion in January 1921 owing to a set of fantastic circumstances when everything went wrong at the same time at this little station in the Upper Severn Valley. One of the contributing factors was that the wrong tablet was handed to a driver by a relief boy porter who could not read.

Here we see a former Great Western Manor, No. 7819 *Hinton Manor,* travelling from Abermule towards Newtown in April 1963 with a stopping train.

Sonning   Pl. 127

This picture could have been taken in 1933 had colour photography of this quality been possible then. It was actually taken in April 1963, in Sonning Cutting – that masterpiece of Brunel on the Great Western main line between Maidenhead and Reading – and shows No. 7008, *Swansea Castle,* heading an up express from Worcester to Paddington at 60 m.p.h. The first coach is still in true Great Western colours, but it was, in fact, repainted this way during the 'Decent Years' (1955-60) when all named Western Region expresses recaptured the spirit of former days.

Longmoor Military Railway Pl. 128

A fairly lengthy stretch of line in Hampshire running from Borden in the north to Liss in the south was maintained and operated by the Royal Army Transportation Corps. It was known as the Longmoor Military Railway, and served to train Army personnel to drive and run railways in the event of their occupying foreign lands. It stood the British Army in great stead during two World Wars when they needed to do just that. Longmoor Downs was the main station on a line 17 miles long, but there was a figure of eight system on which expresses could keep going for four hours or more.

In its latter days, the Longmoor became, frankly, a hobby site for Army people interested in railways. For many it was a paradise posting. Sadly, it came under the Ministry of Defence hammer at the end of 1969; but it may yet become a Museum of operating railway transport, for many engines are stored on it. The custom was for the public to be admitted to an 'open day' each summer, for 6d. a head, and to enjoy footplate rides for larger sums. The picture shows a scene during the last 'open day', 5 July 1969, with the former War Department 2–10–0 locomotive *Gordon*, built in 1943, hauling a train of typical ex-South Eastern and Chatham 'birdcage' non-corridor carriages.

Aberdeen Pl. 129–133

The main line from Aberdeen to Perth and Glasgow remained steam-worked until 1966, providing Scotland with its last express runs behind steam power. Oddly enough, it was one of the first lines to be dieselised, in the mid-'50s, when North British Locomotive Company Type 2 units were put on to trains for the 153-mile journey. They were such an abject failure – and largely contributed to the ultimate bankruptcy of the magnificent locomotive builders who had for so long built steam power for the whole world – that they were replaced by steam engines. In 1962, the wonderful A4 Gresley streamliners, built in 1937 and displaced from the London-Edinburgh main line by Deltic diesels, were sent to Aberdeen (Ferryhill Shed) for working expresses to Glasgow. They were given the fastest schedules ever attempted, three hours for the 153 miles (some of the distance being difficult), inclusive of stops at Stonehaven, Forfar, Perth, and Stirling. Trains never went back to diesel working, for the main line was closed in 1966 between its junction at Kinnaber and Perth General, Glasgow trains being re-routed via Dundee and Perth.

But in May 1965, the scene at Aberdeen was still steamy, with some of the best engines in Britain at work. In plate 129 is a view looking south from Aberdeen Joint Station towards Ferryhill. A Class 5 4-6-0 waits at the head of the 5 p.m. train to Glasgow while A4 4-6-2 No. 60024, *Kingfisher,* backs down to take the 5.15 p.m. semi-fast to Perth. As she came under the great gantry, interested passengers might well have wondered why such a fast and powerful engine should be rostered for the semi-fast instead of the three-hour express. The reason was that several members of the Fleet Street Railway Circle (a group of prominent journalists concerned with railways) were to ride in relays on *Kingfisher's* footplate. As she was not fitted with a corridor tender, it was necessary for the members, two at a time, to change places at station stops. I was among them, and my footplating was done from Stonehaven to Laurencekirk.

Plate 130 shows *Kingfisher,* specially cleaned for the occasion and gleaming in the bright May 1 sunshine, at the head of her comparatively light train a few minutes before departure from Aberdeen.

Photographer Tony Hudson had had the first stint on the footplate, and his camera records plates 131, 132 and 133. Leaving Aberdeen the signal gantry shows through the spectacle glass of *Kingfisher* as the Gresley Pacific, driven by the then Chief Inspector from Ferryhill and aided in firing by the regular fireman and a Fleet Street Railway Circle member, finds her feet. Before long, the locomotive was hurtling down towards Stonehaven along the wild clifftops of the North East Scottish coast at more than 80 m.p.h., faster than the normal limit on this stretch. In the lower picture we see the glowing furnace, which was kept roaring all the way to Perth, where *Kingfisher* came off and went to Perth Shed for turn-round. The train made all the stops and they had to be long ones, for *Kingfisher* gained so much time she was 22 minutes early at Forfar. The final $32\frac{1}{2}$ miles from Forfar to Perth took just under 30 minutes, and an average of 82 m.p.h. was attained for 14 consecutive miles. This rather special occasion was provided by the courtesy of the Scottish Region, whose General Manager at the time, Mr (formerly Brigadier) W. G. Thorpe, is now Deputy Chairman of the British Railways Board.

168

Hereford Pl. 134, 135

From the handsome and unmistakably Great Western station at Hereford a North-South Express pulls away, bound for Pontypool Road, Newport and Cardiff, having come in from Crewe via Shrewsbury. It is 12.42 p.m. on 20 November 1963, and in both pictures No. 7022 *Hereford Castle*, is seen leaving the cathedral city after which she was named, heading into the autumnal afternoon.

Northern Ireland Pl. 136, 137

The last steam locomotives·on public service duties using main lines were the big 2-6-4 tanks of Northern Ireland Railways. They were employed on trains of gravel and spoil between Belfast and Green Island until the end of the summer of 1970, and very occasionally two of them together worked an unusually heavy Belfast-Larne Boat Express on Saturdays. Sadly, these engines were digging their own graves, for the policy of Northern Ireland has been dead set against railways for many years and owing to external pressures enormous amounts of money were spent on motorway construction. These spoil trains, which could be seen many times a day on the shores of Belfast Lough, were carrying material for the motorway which, when completed, would kill the very line on which they travelled.

The Derby-built 2-6-4 tanks, known locally as 'Jeeps', were the last surviving engines of the railways of Northern Ireland apart from those in the Belfast Transport Museum and in private hands. We see No. 66 in plate 136, hauling spoil, and obviously in poor condition since a good deal of unburned fuel is coming out of the chimney. The lower picture shows No. 10 going towards Larne at Ballygarry station, 15 miles from Belfast.

France, Rouen Pl. 138–141

Steam traction survived in France and managed to last until 1972, but few, if any, services for passengers were steam-worked. The situation was very different in 1965, when many main lines had steam expresses, some of them averaging well over 60 m.p.h. despite heavy loads.

Before the overhead electric wires reached from Paris to Rouen and northwards to the Channel coast at Le Havre, the region around Rouen was alive with steam. At the great Sotteville Shed and repair works, a hundred engines could be seen in steam any day of the week. In 1965 Sotteville had, like its fellow Sheds at Calais and Boulogne, Longeau and Nevers, become a tourist attraction, and the rail fans came in their thousands. As many as 800 from Britain have, on a single day, been shown around these Sheds, and even the French started to arrive in order to find out what they were missing. The 'Société des Amis des Chemins du Fer' doubled its membership each year from 1965 onwards, while its opposite number in Germany is going from strength to strength (aided by the German Federal Railways' decision to retain steam in good condition at least until 1975).

Here at Sotteville we see a powerful Canadian-built 1-4-1 R (2-8-2) simmering in front of an ex-Etat Pacific 2-3-1 D. Plate 139 shows a husky 1-5-0 P of the former Nord system (a 2-10-0 of advanced design considering she was built some 26 years before the picture was taken). And in plate 140 one of the ex-Etat thoroughbred Pacifics fresh in from a fast run bringing an express from Paris.

These pictures were taken during an exceptionally hot and sunny October day in 1965, and although the bells were already tolling for Sotteville and steam traction on the lines from Paris (St Lazare) to the coast, all Shed men were keen and hardworking, maintaining their considerable stud of engines, and the visitors from other Sheds, in excellent condition. It always helped, of course, that in France the fireman was responsible for the cleanliness of the tender; this only left the engine herself to be cleaned by Shed staff under the eager supervision of the driver.

Plate 141 depicts a traditional French railway scene, with a Paris Express waiting at Rouen (Rive Droite) Station. This, in fact, tells quite a story, for photographer Hudson shot this picture as I climbed aboard the engine to ride the *marche-pied* (French equivalent of footplate) to Paris with the regional Inspector, a driver and fireman from Le Havre depot, and a colleague from the London *Evening News*, Mr Stuart Friend. Tony Hudson travelled in the first compart- ment of the first coach, recording the journey up the Seine to the French capital.

The engine is Pacific 231G No. 763, of the Depôt du Havre, one of a stud built in 1912 in France and Scotland. This particular one hailed from the North British Locomotive Company in Glasgow. Many hundreds of these Pacifics were built, all of advanced design for the period, and despite modifications and improvements through the years, remained original to the end.

No. 763 came in from Le Havre with the early afternoon restaurant car express (*rapide* is the French word) to Paris, and we joined the train at 14.22 hours. Arrival at Paris (St Lazare) was scheduled for 15.50, giving a time of 88 minutes for the $87\frac{1}{4}$ miles, almost 60 m.p.h. average on a curving road with a heavy (500-ton) train. There were at that time two faster *rapides*, both lighter, one taking 85 minutes and the other 80 minutes, the latter holding pride of place during the 1964–66 period as the world's fastest steam train. How were the mighty fallen, even then, one must reflect – for in 1932 the Great Western Railway held this title with their 'Cheltenham Flyer' running the 77 miles from Swindon to Paddington in 65 minutes, and in 1939 the Milwaukee Railroad in Mid-West America had their 'Hiawatha' averaging 84 m.p.h. between two points on the run between Milwaukee and Minneapolis.

On our trip speed was officially limited to 120 kilometres per hour (74 m.p.h.) which we exceeded only slightly on one occasion. The lighter, faster *rapides* were allowed another 10 km.p.h., close to the maximum approved for the veteran Pacifics with their 6 ft 4 in. driving wheels. I recall the long hard climb through Rolleboise Tunnel (two miles and a bit) at the start of the run, the glorious views of the Seine in summer-like weather as we crossed and re-crossed it, and the hard work of Fireman Chavatte as he supported Driver Dupont in the smooth running of the engine. The two men had been friends for many years, came from Havre Depot, and had worked No. 763 for a decade. The *esprit de corps* they displayed was very common in steam days on French main lines, and both men viewed with regret the changeover to electric or diesel traction planned for early 1967. Anyway, on this fine run on 5 October 1965, the best in French steam performance was presented to us and to several hundred passengers who were deposited at Gare St Lazare at 15.49 hours, a minute ahead of time. Quite a few of the passengers streaming past towards the exits glanced quizzically at the crowded cab of their engine where five goggled and smut-smeared men talked animatedly . . .

France, Cathedrals of Steam   Pl. 142–145

When the Railway Age began to develop it created the largest and most magnificent works of man ever seen except for the medieval castles and cathedrals. Railway builders were conscious of their powerful role in the world and their impact upon the minds of people to whom big things were associated with spiritual and religious bodies. The works of the nineteenth-century railway constructors were, and still are, marvels deserving the highest respect and admiration. In France many railway lines were built by British engineers, particularly Joseph Locke, but later on great French engineers and architects lent their imagination and ability to the projects. Eiffel, for example, learned all his skill on the railways, flinging new steel bridges of stylish pattern across gorges and rivers, before turning to his Parisian spectacular.

But fifty years before Eiffel, the great Paris terminal stations were rising, supreme and graceful, works of art as much to be admired as the earlier cathedrals (it is now only the long-haired or snobbish 'arties' who have not yet admitted this fact). We have heard London stations described as 'Temples of Steam' and 'Monuments to the Steam Age', but in Paris three stations, at least, are often called 'Cathedrals of Steam'. The Gare de Lyon, Gare de l'Est and the Gare du Nord are among the very best in the world. Hittorf was architect for the Nord and Duquisny the Est.

In plates 142 and 143 we see the beautiful Gare de Lyon, a magnificent terminus in French Imperial Chateau style built for the Paris, Lyon, Mediterranée Railway (P.L.M.). The view by night is perhaps even more impressive than by day. From this great station expresses leave for the south and south-east, and also for central and south-east Europe. For over fifty years it saw the departure of the famous 'Simplon Orient Express', and now handles the run-down 'Direct Orient' with its twice-weekly *wagon-lit* to Istanbul. All services using the Gare de Lyon today are electric.

In plate 144 is the Gare de l'Est, terminus of the former Chemin de Fer de l'Est. Although it never had, and still hasn't, much of a suburban service, it possesses some 28 platforms with lines radiating east and north-east. Some say it was laid out like that after Paris began rebuilding following the disastrous Franco-Prussian War of 1870 – all lines leading towards Alsace-Lorraine and Germany to help troops move quickly forward in any war of recovery. As things turned out, the Germans came again, but everyone credits the Gare de l'Est with saving Verdun. From its radiating tracks more than a million troops travelled to Verdun or the nearest railhead, and during the whole of the 1914-18 war it handled some 20,000 troop trains. Today it is fairly quiet, but has expresses to Germany and Switzerland, and sees off the real 'Orient Express' every night on its journey to Stuttgart, Munich, Vienna and Budapest. The last steam engines have gone from its many platforms, but express services to Basle were steam-hauled until 1965. One of the most luxurious restaurants in all Paris occupies much of the first floor of the terminal façade, honoured by three stars in the Michelin Guide.

The Gare du Nord (plate 145) has for a century or more been the first sight of Paris for generations of British travellers. The buses in the wide streets outside are so typical of the city that many first-time travellers gasp with amazement at the pictures coming true. An elderly open-end Paris bus can be seen in this picture. Hurrying travellers often do not pause to admire the magnificent statuary which graces the outside of the station – each statue from Britannia onwards symbolising a place served from the Gare du Nord and the former Chemin de Fer du Nord which owned it. The station sends trains to Boulogne and Calais and Dunkirk (for Channel crossings), to Lille, and to Belgium and Holland. It is the home of the famous 'Night Ferry' Paris-London sleeping car train. The suburban services are considerable, and some of them were still steam-hauled in 1970, using a fascinating pull-and-push high-speed system. The 'Golden Arrow' leaves from here for Calais and Dover every morning; until January 1969, this train was steam-hauled by Pacifics from Amiens onwards to the French coast.

France, Paris Pl. 146-149

The evening rush hour at the Gare du Nord still offered a scene of steam in action until very recently, but at the beginning of 1971 all suburban services were converted to electricity. Here we see – in plate 146 – two steam-hauled trains about to leave for the northern suburbs. The engines are 2-8-2 tanks (Class 141T) fitted with Cossart high-speed reversing gear. They always ran so that they stood outside the overall roof of the Gare du Nord, and on reaching their destinations the drivers walked to the other end of the train and operated the controls by compressed air, while the fireman remained in the cab of the locomotive. It was a similar system to that devised on British branch lines at the turn of the century, but had been developed for much longer and heavier trains with speeds up to and sometimes exceeding 60 m.p.h.

Plate 147 shows two pull-and-push trains ready to depart with one coming into the station under propulsion.

There used to be an intensive steam suburban and main-line service out of St Lazare Station, terminus of the former 'Etat' (State) Railway, a 1908 take-over from the ailing Western of France. Steam push-and-pulls, similar to those operated from the Gare du Nord, ran frequently, intermingled with local third-rail electrics. It was steam to the French coast, all the way, until the beginning of 1967. To handle the large numbers of engines working these trains, a big modern Shed, called Batignolles, was situated less than a mile from St Lazare and within sight of the heights of Montmartre. A view taken in October 1965 (plate 148) shows us Batignolles as it was until very recently, with two Etat 231 D and 231 G Pacifics, plus tanks of 2–8–2 wheel arrangement.

A charming little Shed in the nearer suburbs of Paris was the Vincennes Railway's Nogent Depot, close to the River Seine and about six miles from the odd, and often overlooked, Gare de la Bastille (or Gare de Vincennes as it was officially known). Here lived 22 tank engines of 1914 vintage, all equipped for pull-and-push working, and transferred from the Chemin de Fer de l'Est after early electrification had rendered them redundant on some lines out from the Gare de l'Est. The Shed at Nogent disappeared early in 1970 and with it went the Gare de la Bastille and the whole steam railway. The new Paris regional express Métro took over most of the line to Vincennes except for the last three miles into Paris. Plate 149 shows Nogent Depot in its wooded surroundings, with a number of 2–8–2 tanks getting ready for what used to be a relatively busy evening rush hour. The photograph was taken on 9 May 1966.

France, 'Mountains'   Pl. 150–153

Largest and latest steam passenger locomotives to be built in France, the 2–4–1 P Class 4–8–2s were known as 'Mountains' because of their enormous size. In the curious 'Franglais' idiom, they used the English word, and never applied the French '*Montagne*' to the engines. These big engines with their exceptionally long boilers came on the scene in 1949, and by the end of construction in 1951, some 35 were gracing the S.N.C.F. steam scene. They were used on main-line trains to Marseilles from Dijon, and later Lyon, prior to electrification; then they moved to two areas, Le Mans for Brittany, and Nevers for central France. At the time of writing (in the spring of 1974), although the class is officially withdrawn, about four survive in good working order and are expected to go into action when called upon to rescue diesels failing on Paris-Clermont-Ferrand, or Le Mans-Angers-Nantes trains. French diesels are not necessarily more reliable than those which have cost British Railways so dearly.

Tony Hudson's pictures show 'Mountains' at two places, Nevers Shed and Vichy. In plate 151, No. 2 of the class stands outside the great Shed at Nevers (where 135 steam engines were shedded in 1966 and where over 90 can still be found). The date was 1966 but a new turntable was being built to accommodate additional 'Mountains' on transfer from Brittany following electrification to Rennes. A capital expenditure of this kind shows that French logic is not so far in advance of British when it comes to some railway matters.

On the opposite page, the morning *rapide* from Vichy ('World Capital of Liver' and most famous of the French spas) leaves the station at 9.15 a.m. on 11 May 1966 behind 'Mountain' Class 2-4-1 P No. 3. The heavy train would continue behind this engine until an electric took over at Montereau, 28 miles from the Gare de Lyon.

Switzerland   Pl. 154, 155

The first country in Europe to electrify all its main lines, Switzerland may seem an unexpected place in which to find steam in action. But the Swiss have recognised the commercial value of having a few working steam engines around the country and now boast several lines where people can ride behind them. The last Swiss Federal railway route to go under the wires was in the Ticino in 1961, but private lines continue to use steam for tourism and until 1967 a big 2-10-0 stood by for emergency work at the Swiss Federal Shed in Zurich.

The Swiss are always ready and willing to re-steam a train given an incentive, and such an occasion was provided by the visit of the Sherlock Holmes Society of London to Switzerland in May 1968, re-enacting the Reichenbach Falls encounter. Following in the footsteps of Holmes's creator, Sir Arthur Conan Doyle, a journey was made from Davos to Chur. For this, Rhaetian Railways put on one of their two 2-6-0 tender engines (No. 107) and the special train of four- and six-wheelers was hauled through Klosters and down the Valley to Chur, a two-hour trip with the costumes delighting all onlookers.

Chile   Pl. 156, 157

Little known to most Europeans, the southern part of Chile is one of the finest scenic areas in the world and has a potential for tourism which may not be exploited for at least two decades. At present only the Chilean State Railways do any work for the promotion of tourism, and their famous longitudinal railway running straight down the country from Santiago to Puerto Montt is a line maintained at high standards. Three express trains go down the line every day, the fastest doing the 676 miles in 17 hours. Various branch lines run off the longitudinal main line, westwards to the Pacific coast and eastwards into the great Cordilleras and volcanoes of the Andes. The main line is electrified to Chillan, more than 200 miles south of Santiago, but the branches are steam-worked.

One such branch line goes off to the east from Loncoche Junction for 28 miles to Villarica, a few miles from the gorgeous cone of Pucon volcano. It was from Loncoche Junction, after arriving by the express train 'Fleccia del Sul' (Southern Arrow) that Tony Hudson and I embarked on the branch train for Villarica. The scene was period mid-west America, with clerestoried coaches and worn plush seats, three of them behind a handsome 4–6–0 which at first glance looked like a Baldwin but turned out to be a British product of 1913 (North British Locomotive Company). Our engine made a leisurely trip through sparsely-populated Indian country, stopping at passing loops and stations to let other passenger and freight traffic go through to Loncoche. But once we had reached the summit of the line our driver really let fly and the gallant veteran up front took her train up to 68 m.p.h., thundering down to Villarica, with the great volcano looming up ahead, to arrive three minutes early. So much so that the Land Rover meeting us from the Chilean Railways hotel at Pucon, anticipating the usual five minutes' late arrival, was not to be seen when we alighted from the train. This gave ample time for Tony Hudson to operate his camera and to record this excellent picture of 4–6–0 No. 591 on the morning of 11 March 1966 (plate 156).

Below it is a nostalgic and romantic scene taken just before departure from Villarica towards midnight the next evening as we were waiting for the last branch train to take us to Loncoche and a main-line express to the north.

Kenya   Pl. 158-161

One country which owes its very existence, its actual foundation, to the steam locomotive is Kenya. There were, of course, various tribes living in this large area of East Africa before the Uganda Railway was built up from the Indian Ocean to reach a point in the middle of the Athi Plains in 1900. But the coming of the railway brought cohesion, and a name to the land. It also gave a name to the construction camp – Nairobi (the Cold Well). Today this city is the greatest metropolis in East Africa, the capital of an independent republic, and a modern city with excellent amenities – yet so close to wild life that on any quiet night the roar of lions can be heard at the railway station.

Despite intensive airline services and good roads, Nairobi still depends for its basic supplies on the single thread of railway line coming up from the coast to its site a mile above sea level; and steam engines thundering up the metre gauge still haul the bulk of those supplies, even if diesels have taken over the crack passenger trains.

In 1964, after riding the overnight express up the 320 miles of line from Mombasa to Nairobi, Tony Hudson and I spent some hours in the sunshine of the capital's busy station. In plates 158 and 159 we see a Tribal Class 2-8-4 tender locomotive, No. 2902 *Bukusu*, fitted with a Giesl ejector by the famous Austrian steam engineer. These engines are based on a design for the Nigerian Railways known there as the River Class, and were built by North British Locomotive Company from 1952 to 1954. A total of 31 was supplied to the East African Railways and Harbours Board (successors to the old Uganda Railway). Small wheels (only 4 feet in diameter for the drivers) on a narrow gauge (one metre) do not mean small engines, and some of the East African locomotives are as heavy as any standard-gauge machines in the world. The Tribals are mainly used on the Kenya to Uganda section of the line and here *Bukusu* is starting away in the up-country direction, watched by a crowd of appreciative Kenyan enthusiasts as she passes under an admirably sited spotters' bridge.

Plate 161 shows a very handsome veteran of the Twenty-Four Class, shining in her red livery, one of a few survivors dating from an express type introduced in 1924 and now used on shorter freight and parcels workings.

Plate 160 is of a vintage carriage of the Uganda Railway with a remarkable history. Brought from service in India, where it was built, the coach provided sleeping accommodation for four passengers and was used on construction trains in 1899 and 1900. Once the line had pushed through to Nairobi, Superintendent of the Line Ryall used it as his personal inspection saloon-sleeper. The history of the Uganda Railway is marked by encounters with savage man-eating lions, one group of which held up construction work at Tsavo for four months, leading to statements in the House of Lords by the then British Prime Minister, Lord Salisbury. The 'Man-Eaters of Tsavo', finally disposed of by Colonel Patterson after 28 Indian coolies, three Europeans, and an unknown number of local tribal Africans had been eaten, feature in several classic books.

Lions never gave up the fight against the iron intruder, and early trains were often attacked in the Tsavo-Voi area by angry carnivores hurling themselves against the coaches. One even crashed through into the restaurant car (wooden-built in those days, with flimsy slatted windows) of the mail train in 1901. As late as 1961 there were reports of lions strolling the platform at Voi and holding up a train, while the following year a rhinoceros charged a locomotive head-on, killing itself but derailing the huge Garrett. In late 1900, though, more man-eaters were reported in unexpected areas, and a party of three men, including Superintendent Ryall, decided to try and hunt them. Their sleeper was parked in a siding for the night with one man keeping watch, the window open, listening for any lion sounds outside. Some say he fell asleep, but the next the three men knew was that a man-eater had jumped into the sleeper among them. It savaged the watchkeeper, then dragged poor Ryall out of the carriage, eating him in view of his shocked companions.

A re-enactment of this grisly scene was undertaken with a tame lion and a dummy for the film *Permanent Way*, made for the East African Railways in 1963. The same sleeping car was used, for it had been preserved on Nairobi station as a monument to the men who lost their lives building the railway. The author of this book, notebook in hand, stands beside it in the picture, taken on 18 June 1964.

Uganda   Pl. 162–165

Although the Uganda Railway achieved its objective early in 1901 by reaching the shores of Lake Victoria, where a pre-fabricated steamer took passengers and goods across to Kampala (Port Bell), it was not for another 30 years that rails actually appeared on Uganda territory. The line was built beyond Nakuru over the Highlands to the Uganda border, then down past Jinja at the source of the Nile to Kampala itself. On this journey, the railway reaches a height of over 9,000 feet at the equator, the highest point attained by any main-line railway in the British Commonwealth.

The 'Uganda Mail' heads up-country from Nairobi at 9.15 a.m., to reach Kampala 24 hours later. Steam is still in action on the stretches beyond Eldoret in the Kenya Highlands, although diesels have gone right through to Kampala. In 1963, however, steam took over at Nakuru in Kenya and with only one change of engine (at Eldoret) went to the Uganda capital. On a journey which Tony Hudson and I made in the 'Uganda Mail' in January 1963, we were awakened in a very civilized and comfortable fashion by the attendant bringing a pot of tea at 6.30 a.m., pulling up the window shutters, and revealing a dawn lighting up the very source of the Nile. But just as we had finished dressing and were about to go along to the restaurant car for breakfast, the 'Uganda Mail' reduced its normal 25 to 30 m.p.h. gait to walking pace, and the gruesome spectacle shown in plates 164 and 165 met our eyes. Tony Hudson's camera reveals the devastating effects of an unusual railway disaster which had occurred a few days before, on 3 January 1963, just 23 miles from Kampala.

A goods train travelling at night towards Kampala had stalled on the steep gradient despite the powerful 60 Class Beyer-Garrett locomotive No. 60025, *Sir Henry Colville* (named after a former Governor of the East African countries). The train consisted of six tankers of high octane aviation fuel (bound for Entebbe Civil Airport) followed by four goods trucks and a guard's van. A set back was started, then the driver opened up his engine and made a run at the gradient, breasting it easily and tearing down the other side. The locomotive derailed with all its tanks, and escaping fuel was ignited by the oil furnace on the engine. A tremendous explosion resulted as 175,000 gallons of fuel went up and the subsequent blaze lit up Kampala. Both enginemen, Africans, were killed, and were later buried communally, being unidentifiable, but the guard's van and one truck escaped the fire. More than 100 workmen had the line open again after three days of continuous round-the-clock effort. And to point up how sturdy a steam locomotive is, plate 162 shows the same engine a year later (at Kasese in Western Uganda) looking none the worse for her roasting. She was, in fact, fully restored to working order in a little over three months.

Plate 163 shows a strong steamy scene in the African dawn; the 'Uganda Mail', now 463 miles out of Nairobi and 31 miles from Kampala, takes water as a freight train stands on the loop. Both engines are Beyer-Garretts, a 58 Class on the 'Mail' to the left with her oil furnaces roaring, and a 60 Class on the right. The station is Kawolo, about 3,550 feet above sea level. The 58 Class were unnamed but the 60 in the picture is No. 60021, *Sir Wm. Gowers.*

Czechoslovakia   Pl. 166–171

Nowhere in Europe is modern steam power so readily visible as in Czechoslovakia. The Czech State Railways (C.S.D.) have a fleet of some 3,000 steam engines, all well maintained and effective. Nearly all of them have been fitted with Dr Giesl's famous ejector, the oblong chimney that improves thermal efficiency. While Czech Railways are making rapid advances with electric traction, many main-line trains are steam-hauled and a great deal of suburban work around Prague and Bratislava is undertaken with steam traction.

On a visit in September 1967, Tony Hudson and I secured that much sought-after and ultimate privilege, a joint footplate pass. This enabled us to ride on the train engine of the double-headed 'Balt-Orient Express' between Cseska Trebova and Brno, a distance of 53 miles. Having travelled as passengers from Prague in the express, which was electric-hauled as far as Cseska Trebova in Moravia, we changed to the footplate armed with our documents and rode with the driver, a well-educated young man with a degree, married to a lady doctor. This was a run with problems, for a bad derailment had occurred early that morning at Svitavy when a semi-fast passenger train jumped the points, crashed into the station buildings and killed four people.

This meant only one line was clear on the way to Brno and explains the curious and frightening situation shown in plate 167. 'Wrong line' working was in force over double track sections before and after Svitavy and in this instance two trains, one of them ours, were dashing along parallel tracks in the same direction. Later the situation returned to normal and other views on this page show the train swinging round a curve as seen from the footplate and a train coming the other way hauled by a British-built 2–10–0 (delivered just after the war for freight work in liberated countries).

In plate 170 we see the 'Balt-Orient Express' arrived at Brno, with the leading engine, No. 498.035, a 4–8–2 of the latest type, standing well down the platform. I am saying farewell in halting, broken German to the driver, but in fact we were to meet him again at Bratislava, when visiting the fascinating engine shed. The picture below was irresistible – a typical 'dignity and impudence' set-up with an Albatross Class 475 4–8–2 dating from the late 1950s alongside the Depot 'pug' 0–6–0 tank. The red stars carried by Soviet Bloc engines can be seen on the 475, but during the brief period of Czech liberalism (in 1968) they were removed.

Hungary   Pl. 172–175

If Czechoslovakia enters the '70s as the active steam paradise of Europe, Hungary can claim to have offered the railway enthusiast of the mid-'60s an abundance of locomotive sights and sounds and types. Veterans nearly a century old mingled with modern steam power, and in the Hungarian capital, one terminal station – Nyugati – could boast five steam trains drawn up for departure with a different class of locomotive on each.

Diesel and electric traction, most of the equipment provided by the Soviet Union, has made deep inroads on the Hungarian railway scene. But M.A.V. (Hungarian State Railways) still have considerable numbers of steam engines in action. Among them are nearly 200 4–8–0s of the 424 Class, high-boilered and red-starred, regarded as the most useful steam locomotives at work in central Europe. Occasionally one can see very elderly 0–6–0 tender engines with outside springs and low boilers, known to Hungarian railwaymen as 'Szarás Kaçjàs' (hairy ducks) from their curious waddling motion. They date from a design introduced in 1862 and a few veterans shunting in the Budapest area are nearly one hundred years old.

Late in August 1965 Tony Hudson's camera captured views of a modern 424 Class engine hauling a fast freight between Budapest and Lake Balaton (plate 172) and a 'hairy duck' 0–6–0 working on the outskirts of Budapest near Ferihegy (plate 173). There is a difference in age between these locomotives of about 90 years.

A few years before the Second World War the then Royal Hungarian State Railways built two streamlined 4–4–4 tank engines of a very unusual design. With their large-diameter driving wheels they had an amazing turn of speed and one of them – No. 242 – recorded 177 kilometres per hour with a light train (equivalent to $109\frac{1}{2}$ m.p.h.). At the beginning of the 1960s these interesting tank locomotives were rostered to haul in tandem the famous 'Balt-Orient Express' from Budapest to the Romanian frontier. During our 1965 visit we learned that, while No. 241 had been withdrawn, No. 242 was still working occasionally although scheduled for preservation and was based at Püspökladány, junction for Romania on the line to Debreçen. The railway authorities in Budapest, puzzled at first by our interest in and knowledge of what they called 'this relic', agreed to have the engine taken out of the shed and steamed for us. The result can be seen in plates 174 and 175. Although in steam and obviously fit for duty, No. 242 only moved in and out of the shed and took water. We were unable to persuade the shedmaster to roster her for a local turn from Püspökladány to Debreçen and back. It is pleasing to know that this engine is now securely preserved in the Budapest Transport Museum's outstation.

Yugoslavia   Pl. 176, 177

Sunny Yugoslavia with its rugged mountains and gorgeous sea coast is a land sparsely served by railways due to difficult terrain and late development. It was not until 1869 that a line reached Belgrade, and in those days the Ottoman Turks – who had occupied the land sleepily for about 400 years – were still in power there, though confined to the Kalamegdan fortress from which they were ousted the next year. The northern parts of 'Great Slavia' were under Austro-Hungarian rule until 1918, and here, in Slovenia and Croatia, some lines were built, mainly to serve garrisons and ports from Vienna. Montenegro was without land transport until quite recently.

As a result, the railways of Yugoslavia grew haphazardly and their tractive power was supplied from various outside sources. A major Shed, such as Zagreb or Ljubljana, might have engines from seven different countries, and to add to the interest, shedmasters were allowed to introduce variations of their own when having local repairs or modifications done. So in the early 1960s the country offered a treat to railway enthusiasts never likely to be exceeded (but today possibly equalled by the situation in North Portugal, where, at Contumil, there are engines from 8 countries).

American diesels have swept into Yugoslavia today and much secondary traffic is now hauled by this means, although most main lines are now electrified. However, there are some secondary lines and even some narrow gauge (near Dubrovnik for example), where steam is still in action. Plates 176 and 177 were taken by Tony Hudson on 30 September 1963, at Zagreb. The top one shows a handsome 2–6–2 in very clean condition coming in with a stopping train from Ljubljana. Built in Berlin in 1912, the engine is No. 22.064 which started life on the Austrian system. The lower picture is of Zagreb Shed, showing four locomotives of various designs and modifications.

Spain   Pl. 178–179

The Spanish railway scene has undergone a fantastic transformation in very recent years, with new electrification being pressed on at great speed, new short-cut lines reducing distances between main cities, and streamlined diesel units flashing about at speeds hitherto unknown on the Iberian peninsula. Bogie-changing systems at the Irun and Port Bou frontiers with France permit through running, with trains linking Paris and Madrid, Geneva and Barcelona, without change of carriage. The new sleeping car express 'Puerta del Sol', running from Paris to Madrid overnight with dinner, bed and breakfast included in the fare, has made deep inroads into the air traffic between those two cities. Leaving Paris at 18.30 it arrives with the same sleepers (still a source of wonder to many Spaniards used to the isolation of their wide gauge) at 09.00 hours. Less than 300 steam engines survive in regular use on the R.E.N.F.E. (Spanish State Railways) system. Those that do are superb.

But in the mid-'60s, Spain was still the happy hunting ground for observers wanting to see and photograph veteran steam in action. Some sheds could produce remarkable specimens lurking in their depths, and in Malaga, Tony Hudson and I found a Belgian-built tank with Cockerill's construction plate on the side showing 1861. Early in 1966, I saw an 0–6–0 tender engine from 1858 shunting outside Seville virtually unaltered. There were, of course, Talgo and TAF diesel and electric trains intermingled with the veterans and big 4–8–2s of post-war construction handling heavy expresses at this time. It was rather a mistake for uninformed observers seeing an ancient shunting engine chuffing along a heavily-grassed Spanish track to assume the railway system was derelict. Good engineers could keep an engine going and in the Spanish climate a veteran can last well, while grass is commonly employed in Mediterranean lands to 'bind' the track in the absence of suitable ballast. Spain was, of course, very poor until the tourism boom, coupled with loans from the World Bank, enabled a great deal of money to be spent on the railway system.

Plates 178 and 179 date from November 1965, near the end of the era of the veterans, and the top one shows a 4-8-0 of 1921 vintage, Class 240 No. 2045 outside Malaga Shed. The lower picture could have been taken half a century before it actually was, or even 70 years ago. It is of a Beyer Peacock 0-8-0 with an Adams smokebox, built in 1892, setting out from Malaga with a light goods train. This is a scene which vanished almost overnight as the '60s drew to a close.

Specials   Pl. 180-182

It is an inevitable human reaction that as soon as a thing we take for granted begins to disappear, there is a wave of emotion about it and millions who appeared disinterested flock to see it. So it was with steam in action and so it still is. During the mid-'60s, the British Railways Board co-operated with the running of special trains hauled by selected engines, and even allowed enthusiasts to clean and help prepare them for the runs. In January 1963, Mr Alan Pegler, a businessman and lifelong railway enthusiast, bought *Flying Scotsman* from British Railways, restored her to L.N.E.R. colours and numbering, signed a contract which enabled him to keep the engine running on U.K. metals for ten years, and put her back to work hauling specials. But with the end of steam in normal service in Britain, which came about in August 1968, the Board clamped down on all specials involving steam traction. It antagonised a large and valuable market, formerly sympathetic to railways, and it tried to end the Pegler contract. This did not succeed and a situation existed, and still exists, whereby Mr Pegler's *Flying Scotsman* is the only steam engine allowed to run on British Railways. There are indications that the Board is tending to soften its attitude, but a few known 'hard-liners' remain obdurate.

The pictures on these pages were taken during the days when steam specials were running all over the country, giving famous and much-loved engines a chance of showing their paces on outings with enthusiast groups. In plates 180 and 181 we see one of the last Stanier Pacifics in active service, No. 46251, *City of Nottingham*, starting away from Woodford Halse on the former Great Central Line with the 'East Midlander', a special run from Marylebone Station in London to Leicester, Nottingham, and Sheffield Victoria. The special was operated by the Railway Correspondence and Travel Society and the date was Saturday, 9 May 1964. Magnificent engines of the Coronation Class introduced in 1937 by Sir William Stanier as enlarged versions of his 1933 Princess Royals, the 'City' Pacifics were mostly streamlined, although their casing was removed from 1946 onwards. However, *City of Nottingham* was built without streamlining just as the Second World War began. A sprinkling of these superb Pacifics survives in various parts of the country, preserved in private hands or by corporations.

Gracing plate 182 is the attractive single driver, Caledonian No. 123, seen here a very long way indeed from her native metals. She stands at Norwood Junction Shed, 410 miles from Glasgow, on 12 September 1963, being serviced for the long journey back to Scotland under her own steam after working some specials on the famous Bluebell Line in Sussex.

During the first five years of the '60s, this admirable engine worked numerous specials in Scotland, hauling two original Caledonian carriages. Both locomotive and rolling stock were painted in Caledonian colours, a regal blue for the former and deep maroon and cream for the latter. No. 123 became celebrated for her incredible performances in the Railway Races to Edinburgh in 1888; for 23 consecutive days she took the express from Carlisle to Glasgow ($100\frac{1}{2}$ miles) in timings ranging from $102\frac{1}{2}$ to 110 minutes when the schedule called for 112 minutes. This route includes the tremendous climb over Beattock Summit, 10 miles of 1 in 70 to 1 in 80, which she cleared with an 80-ton load at $37\frac{1}{2}$ m.p.h. On level track No. 123 travelled at a steady 73 to 75 m.p.h., the upper limit of speed in the eighties. Apart from a brief period during the Railway Races to Aberdeen of 1895, no train ascended Beattock so rapidly for another 45 years.

This remarkable engine was designed by Dugald Drummond and built as a 'one-off' job in two months by Neilson & Company in Glasgow. In fact, from receipt of the order to her delivery for display at the Edinburgh Exhibition of 1886 was only 66 days. Her fame grew nationwide after the '88 Races, when photographs of her, and even her driver and his family, appeared in national newspapers. From 1900 to 1923 she was chosen by the Caledonian Railway to act as Royal Pilot Engine, running ahead of Royal Specials, and when not thus employed she hauled the Directors' inspection saloon. Later, in L.M.S.R. colours, she returned to passenger work, hauling trains between Perth and Dundee until 1935, by which time she was the last single driver at work in the British Isles. Today No. 123 may be admired in the Glasgow Transport Museum.

Condemned   Pl. 183, 184

There have always been graveyards for steam engines, and it was always felt by those who ascribe living qualities to iron horses that an engine which 'died' at the shed where it had been based had had a good 'life'. Longevity is characteristic of steam locomotives, especially goods engines, and 50 years was not an unusual life for the latter. Even hard-worked fast express engines averaged 30 years. But when the total slaughter began in 1955 after the White Paper announced the doom of steam, engines were ruthlessly cut down in their prime and often condemned in sheds, and even on regions, which were not their own. Accountants, by a stroke of the pen, destroyed hundreds, and indeed thousands, of engines with years of useful work in them, replacing them with a tractive product that has proved costly and frequently unreliable.

In the 1960s long lines of forlorn engines became a common sight, and many hundreds can still be seen awaiting the torch at scrap yards in Wales, the North East, and Norfolk. But, as can be seen in plates 183 and 185, two at least are dying where they were born. In the top picture *King Charles 1st*, No. 6010 of the famous Great Western Railway King Class, built at Swindon in 1927, is seen awaiting cutting-up at Swindon in May 1964. The lower picture is of Schools Class No. 30923 *Bradfield*, one of the 40 superb 4-4-0s built by the Southern Railway to Maunsell's design between 1930 and 1932. Born at Eastleigh in 1931, *Bradfield* is seen on the condemned row at Eastleigh in August 1963.

Saved   Pl. 185, 186

First of the Great Western 'Kings' was No. 6000, *King George V*, built in 1927 and the most powerful 4-6-0 of her time. Within months of completion this magnificent engine was sent to the United States to take part in the Baltimore and Ohio Railway's centenary celebrations. She was fitted with a bell for her runs in America and many legends have grown up about her turn of speed while hauling American coaches.

The Kings worked the Great Western's heaviest expresses and later those of the Western Region, ending their days on the Paddington to Birmingham line, where between 1958 and 1962 they hauled all the important traffic while electrification work proceeded on the London Midland line from Euston. Many fine runs were performed by these engines, all well over 30 years old at the time, and *King George V* recorded journeys as good as when new. But September 1962 saw the complete withdrawal of the Kings in face of dieselisation of the Birmingham, Wolverhampton and Shrewsbury route. Almost all were withdrawn from service but one or two worked race trains and specials until May 1963 when the last King ran a special trip watched by 80,000 mourning rail fans. No. 6000 was scheduled for preservation and went to Swindon in November 1962 where she was stored in a rather decrepit paint shed. Here she languished unattended for six years, allegedly awaiting a suitable site at Swindon for display in that town's museum. But the Great Western Museum at Swindon, an ethereal place converted from a church, is already completely full and no space is likely to be found for *King George V* until large-scale alterations are made.

Meanwhile, a great railway enthusiast in Herefordshire, Mr Peter Prior, Managing Director of Bulmer's Cider, set about acquiring her and running her on a special train of Pullmans painted in Bulmer's livery. I am glad to have had the privilege of being consulted very early on, and negotiations were subsequently successful, resulting in *King George V* being hauled ceremoniously out of the decaying paint shed by ropes over newly-laid tracks. The people hauling her were thousands, literally thousands, of railway enthusiasts who had turned up in pouring rain to pay their tribute. Completely restored to her pre-war finery by Adams and Sons of Newport, Monmouth, who did an amazing and devoted job, *King George V* came to Hereford in triumph and her arrival was inaugurated in November 1968 at a ceremony at which I was delighted to be present, lunching in one of the Bulmer Pullmans while 'K.G.5' (as she is known to all Hereford people) steamed up and down the Bulmer sidings. British Railways, after taking a churlish attitude, now give permission for this splendid engine to appear again in steam on their lines. I stress 'their lines' because a large and mistaken body of opinion in Britain had thought that after nationalisation they were 'our lines' . . .

Tony Hudson's picture captures the King in splendour at the head of the Bulmer Pullmans steaming at Hereford on 3 August 1969.

Plate 186 shows a reclaimed Southern Schools, not, unhappily, in steam, but preserved at the head of the sort of Pullmans she used to haul so efficiently to Bournemouth. The engine, No. 928 *Stowe* (B.R. number 30928) built in 1931 and withdrawn in 1963, is now owned by Lord Montagu of Beaulieu who is a railway enthusiast as well as a motor fan, and recognises vintage craftsmanship on rail as well as road. The engine, with three Pullmans, stands in the open close to Lord Montagu's Motor Museum. Purists may question the locomotive's livery but all are delighted to see her intact.

The King   Pl. 187

On the footplate of a King – of course it has to be *King George V* because the date is August 1969 and only one survives in working condition. While steaming at Hereford, Tony Hudson captures the scene in the cab with its typical Great Western features – the driver on the right in contrast to other British railways, his left hand on the regulator, right hand on the valve gear.

Many are the stories told by well-known persons who have been on the footplate of a King, especially in steam. A Birmingham editor once headed his story 'The King and I'; a national newspaper came out with 'Regal Power'. But most suitable of all was the *Western Mail*'s headline on the evening of the arrival of *King George V* at Hereford – 'Monarchy Restored'.

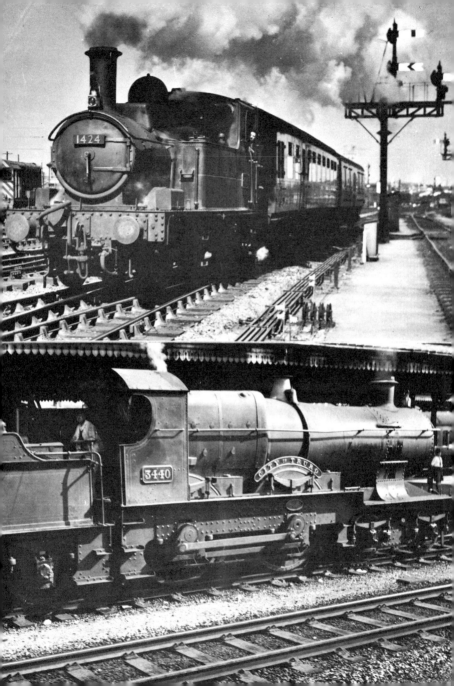